Snorkelling a
Diving in Oman

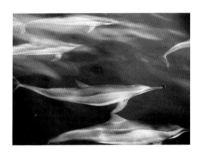

MOTIVATE
PUBLISHING

Snorkelling and Diving in Oman

Rod Salm and Robert Baldwin

Published with the support
and encouragement of

Published by Motivate Publishing

Dubai: PO Box 2331, Dubai, UAE
Tel: (+971 4) 282 4060, fax: (+971 4) 282 0428
e-mail: books@motivate.ae   www.booksarabia.com

Office 508, Building No 8, Dubai Media City, Dubai, UAE
Tel: (+971 4) 390 3550, fax: (+971 4) 390 4845

Abu Dhabi: PO Box 43072, Abu Dhabi, UAE
Tel: (+971 2) 677 2005, fax: (+971 2) 677 0124

London: Acre House, 11/15 William Road, London NW1 3ER
e-mail: motivateuk@motivate.ae

Directors:	Obaid Humaid Al Tayer and Ian Fairservice
Consultant Editor:	David Steele
Deputy Editors:	Moushumi Nandy, Jennifer Evans
Assistant Editor:	Zelda Pinto
Art Director:	Andrea Willmore
Senior Designer:	Cithadel Francisco
General Manager Books:	Jonathan Griffiths
Publishing Coordinator:	Jenny Bateman-Irish

First published 1991
First revised edition 1992
Reprints 1996, 1998
New edition 2007

Photographic credits
Andrea Willmore: 8, 13, 15, 18, 19
Christa Loustalot: 2, 6, 25, 60, 62, 65(t),
68(b), 70(b), 77 (t), 79(t)
(www.photograsea.net)
Moushumi Nandy: 9, 90 (b), 103
Warren R Baverstock: Front cover
(www.verstodigital.com)

Front cover: Scuba divers explore the beauty of Oman's underwater world.
Back cover: Large schools of fusiliers are a common sight near coral reefs in Oman.
Title page: Literally meaning 'naked gill', nudibranchs, like this pair of *Risbecia pulchella*, are the slugs of the sea.

ISBN: 978 1 86063 162 7

British Library Cataloguing-in-Publication Data
A catalogue record for this book is available from the British Library

Printed and bound in the UAE by Al Ghurair Printing Press

CONTENTS

Scuba divers float effortlessly over a reef in Oman's waters.

DIVING EMERGENCIES

Naval Recompression Chamber

24-hour emergency telephone number:
+968 99350587

- This number will connect you with the Duty Diving Officer, Said bin Sultan Naval Base, Wudam. Please ensure you have adequate and up-to-date diving medical insurance, as there will be a cost to use the recompression chamber.

- The Armed Forces Hospital at Al Khoud will accept all diving emergencies and will carry out initial assessment and stabilization prior to transfer to Wudam.

- The emergency wards of both The Royal Hospital and Al Khoula Hospital can deal with stings, cuts, bites, fractures and other injuries. Private hospitals in Muscat, such as the Shatti Hospital and Muscat Private Hospital are also well equipped to deal with such emergencies. Make sure you know the most direct route to these place.

Currents connect the farthest reaches of the oceans into one vast, continuous system. The world's oceans provide most of our oxygen, rainfall, weather and temperature control. Our survival depends on it, yet we know so little about it and so few of us ever have any close contact with it.

We, the snorkelling and diving community, are a privileged few who cross through the inscrutable surface of the sea to marvel at its mysteries. We are often so overwhelmed by what we see that we can become unaware of the impact we have in this most fragile of environments and the sensitive creatures that live within. Each one of us should do what we can to maintain the continued health of the ocean and the great wealth of its resources.

As a start, be alert, caring and responsible when exploring the hidden wonders of the sea and, when you emerge, leave only your stress behind; take away only your excitement, memories and photographs.

Water covers two-thirds of the world, concealing vast plains, basins, gaping canyons, huge mountain ranges, volcanoes and a seemingly endless quantity of plant and animal life, with none more varied than those inhabiting a coral community. Photographs and descriptions can't begin to do justice to the rich variety, colour and abundance of life below sea level. To sense it fully, you must experience it for yourself.

Contrary to their popular image, snorkelling and diving are not 'macho' sports reserved for the fittest, bravest and strongest among us: standing at a cocktail party requires more exertion than effortlessly floating face down over a coral garden. As long as you can float, you can snorkel. Even the weakest of swimmers can find a calm haven to fish-watch in shallow water. As you enter the sea for the first time, you embark on an underwater adventure; the profusion of life, movement and colour will envelop and entice you.

Activities such as snorkelling and diving are easy to pursue in the Sultanate. The water is warm all year round and much of the coast, with its many great underwater sites, is readily accessible. The coast is largely free of pollution and relatively undisturbed by people; in fact, many places along Oman's coastline have yet to be explored underwater. Knowing yours are the first human eyes to view a site conveys a sense of excitement; the observant are rewarded with new species of fish, shells and coral.

This book highlights some of the better-known snorkelling and diving sites round the Sultanate, their locations and points of access, and what to look

A single clownfish nestles in the swollen tentacles of its host anemone.

for when you get there. Other sites are deliberately omitted because they are pristine and fragile; to encourage enthusiasts to visit them might lead to damage or even their demise. Then again, to include too many sites would leave little room for personal exploration with its own unique excitement and rewards. Generally speaking, one can snorkel or dive anywhere along a rocky coast and not be disappointed, so do not feel constrained by the list of sites in the book.

It may strike some as strange that there is no special section on the dangers of the deep or related information on first aid. There are two reasons for this. Firstly, these have already been covered in great detail in three books available in Oman: *The Coral Seas of Muscat, Seashells of Southern Arabia* and *Red Sea Safety*. Secondly and, more importantly, it is our strong belief that

the perils caused by marine animals are exaggerated beyond all proportion: the image of the sea as a place fraught with danger is one deliberately promoted by some divers. Don't be impressed by the tridents, prodders and clubs these people take down to the depths with them. These look as ridiculous as a machete in the hands of someone strolling through a wooded area.

Do not be alarmed by sharks here. Although they are quite abundant, there has never been a recorded case of an attack against a swimmer, snorkeller or diver in Oman. To prove the point, try photographing them up close – they are frustratingly shy – solidifying our belief that the best defence against Oman's sharks is a camera.

A note of warning: if you see anyone spear fishing, stop them if you can. Not only is this activity illegal, but it could cause a shark problem.

Snorkelling in the Musandam region, especially close to the Strait of Hormuz is diverse and exciting, with a varied and colourful array of marine life.

Barracudas should not be feared here. However, you should never wear bright, flashy trinkets when either snorkelling or diving in the sea as barracudas may instinctively rush a swimmer in a response to glinting or glittering objects.

The truly dangerous reef creatures are those armed for their own protection: poisonous fish, stingrays, the spines of sea urchins and the sharp ridges of corals and oysters. The rest, in a long list of armaments, are weapons of defence, not offence, but it is the careless diver who exposes him or herself to these dangers. The rule here: never stand on coral. Not only will you smash their delicate infrastructure and destroy the shelter of innumerable creatures, but you will expose yourself to marine-life booby-traps at the same time – a foot full of sea-urchin spines or stitches in your ankle will certainly stop you in your tracks.

In addition, avoid the urge to touch.

The poison from some cone shells can prove fatal if the shell harpoons a handler, moray eels frequently lurk in holes beside lobsters and will deter further intrusion with a swift bite to a probing hand, and some of the most seemingly innocuous fish have concealed spines and scalpel-sharp barbs or scales, which they are quick to use when trapped or harassed. Divers who traverse the seabed with their hands should remove a few weights and swim instead, to avoid damaging bottom dwellers and themselves at the same time.

Float quietly and attentively over the reefs and the resident sea creatures will offer little trouble, but beware of the blisteringly hot, summer sun: keep well covered. In addition, always check and respect the sea's currents.

Snorkellers, divers, beachcombers and rock-pool potterers are urged to buy the following reference books: *The Coral*

The Musandam Peninsula provides great snorkelling and diving opportunities for tourists in the midst of spectacular landscape.

Hints for boat handlers

Avoid anchoring on coral: your anchor can destroy 50 years of coral growth in five minutes.

- Where possible anchor in sand off the edge of the reef, or look for large white patches of sand in the reef and anchor there.

- If sand patches are small or difficult to find, swim the anchor down and set it in sand by hand.

- Always check the anchor is properly set in sand and that the chain or rope is unlikely to snag coral.

- Find the anchor prior to ascent and ensure that both it and the chain and rope won't snag coral or rocks before attempting to raise it.

Be considerate:

- Keep a sharp lookout for fishermen's floats – and submerged ropes in particular – and give them a wide berth if at all possible.

- Move slowly near popular underwater sites, such as at Bandar Khayran, Bandar Jissah and Fahl Island; underwater noise pollution detracts from your diving and snorkelling pleasure.

- Stay clear of divers' bubbles and remain aware around snorkellers; some of the more accomplished participants can stay submerged for two minutes or more.

Seas of Muscat, Corals Of Oman, The Living Seas, Marine Life of the Southern Gulf, Seashells of Oman or Seashells of Eastern Arabia, Red Sea Invertebrates, Coastal Fishes of Oman, Red Sea Reef Fishes, Sharks of Arabia and Red Sea Safety, which are available throughout the Sultanate. Some publications are also available from the library of the Marine Science and Fisheries Centre. Various reference cards, such as Fishes of the Souk and South Arabian Reef Fishes are also excellent for field use. Laminate them with a half-centimetre edge for underwater use.

Only the common names of the fish, coral and other sea creatures found in this book are used and, in most cases, the names correspond to those used in the field guides mentioned on the previous page. A glossary at the end of the book lists the common names used here and in the field guides, along with their corresponding scientific names.

Our boats can take us to naturally protected areas of wilderness, but we must be careful not to disturb or damage the ocean's pristine character in our attempt to explore its depths. Always bear in mind that access to these sites is not our right, but a privilege that we will only be permitted to enjoy as long as we cause minimal disturbance. Be especially careful to lower your anchor onto sand, then follow the rope down and secure the anchor properly in the sand: boat anchors have been responsible for the destruction of large areas of coral in some parts of the world much frequented by divers and this has ultimately resulted in their closure to further forays. The same is happening at sites around Muscat, such as at Fahl Island so, if you plan to dive this area, be considerate and ensure you preserve its natural state.

The coast of Oman is wild and varied. There is a wealth of scenery, wildlife, opportunity and pleasure awaiting the intrepid underwater explorer. There is also the constant promise of the discovery of new places, things and phenomena. The relative remoteness of sections of the rocky coastline and islands has helped to preserve their natural beauty and wildlife. Consequently, these areas offer dramatic scenery, greater contact with nature and more opportunities for exploratory diving.

The long, rather-dull-for-divers sweep of Batinah Beach yields to the rugged beauty of the rocky coast at Ras al Hamra. From here to beyond Muscat the coast is, with good reason, densely developed. Despite this, you can still find havens of tranquility in several small coves featured on this coast.

The embayed and stable nature of the rocky coasts from Muscat to the border with Yemen, and of Musandam, encourage the growth of corals and/or other colourful marine life, making these particularly valuable areas for snorkelling and scuba diving.

The Muscat area suffers the tantrums of fickle north winter winds that make the sea off limits in all but the most sheltered bays. During May and June the sea settles and warms, producing the clearest of waters, and these are the best months to spend time in the sea.

In summer, the seas of the Muscat area are generally calm and still. The fierce summer sun warms the upper six to 10 metres so that there is a noticeable break or thermocline between this layer and the underlying cold water. Plankton thrives in the warm water, which decreases the chances of good visibility in July, August and September. Nonetheless, the sea offers an excellent refuge from summer's unrelenting heat

and humidity. Beware of sunburn during this season – the temptation to snorkel and dive without a wetsuit may cause overexposure to the severe summer sun.

Complex winds and currents occasionally cause the upwelling of cold water from the depths. This is particularly noticeable in summer when seawater temperatures can drop by as much as 10°C in a day or two. Both summer and winter upwelling are very localized in the Muscat area, and can cause red tides, which colour the sea a bright orange-red.

The Dhofar upwelling is quite different. This is a fairly stable, constant upwelling that continues for four to five months during the *khareef*, or monsoon summer months, a period of tremendously rough, cold, green seas, when seaweed grows and proliferates on all rocky coasts of the southern region. The huge swells and surf ensure that most of this coast is closed for diving. However,

The corals and macroalgae of the Dhofar region are exposed to one of the most unique coral-growing environments.

certain bays and coves are reasonably well sheltered, offering fascinating snorkelling and diving among the seaweed forests. This seaweed grows quickly when upwelling floods the seas with nutrient-rich cool water, and some can reach 1.5 to two metres in length in just a few months.

September is the best time to experience the seaweed forests, as the sea's swell and upwelling have subsided, the sea is warming, but the seaweed has not yet died off. When the seaweed dies, it does so quickly, accumulating in masses that rot in the shallows, making access to some underwater sites a rather unpleasant experience.

Rocky reefs fringe most of the Dhofar Coast, providing a substrate for coral as well as for seaweed communities. Corals are remarkably abundant in some of the sheltered mainland coves and around the Al Hallaniyat Islands, where they form attractive and varied communities. Certain Dhofar corals, fish, seaweed, starfish and sea urchins are found nowhere else in Oman and you will be amazed by the quantity of large and fearless fish. Some of Dhofar's weed-

This cabbage coral seems to sweep out to sea forming surrealistic patterns.

covered reefs are also major feeding grounds for green turtles, and large green and loggerhead turtles are a common sight underwater.

Unfortunately, large patches of dead coral are a common sight and a source of speculation in the Muscat and Musandam areas. The infamous coral predator, the crown-of-thorns starfish, has killed off some of these areas of coral, along with tangled fishing nets and silt-laden floodwaters, which have almost certainly played a significant part in the death of these coral reefs. It is also likely that the summer upwelling contributes to localized coral mortality by sudden, plummeting temperatures, which stress the corals beyond their tolerance levels.

Being comfortable in the water is the key to enjoying snorkelling and diving. Choose your equipment carefully and start off snorkelling at your own pace. Remember, the best snorkellers make the safest divers, so don't allow yourself to be rushed into diving. Diving ties you to heavy and expensive equipment which requires a means to transport it and you'll require a suitable source of compressed air. Safety requirements these days will burden you with enough equipment, so beware of being talked into strapping on every conceivable gadget that opens and shuts. Tried and true equipment is often a better option.

A good snorkeller is truly free of unnecessary equipment. You need no more than a mask, a snorkel, a pair of fins and the time to use them. Many a comfortable snorkeller is content never to dive, even when presented with the option, thanks to the accessibility of the snorkelling experience.

Top tips on what to look for when buying snorkelling equipment follow; places to buy or service equipment are listed in the appendix.

Masks

1. Choose a mask that fits. To test this, put the mask over your face without donning the strap. Inhale lightly, let go and if the mask remains in place, it seals well. A good seal is most important!
2. Check the mask has the following:
   a. a double seal where it presses against the face for a better fit and comfort during your snorkel/dive
   b. tempered or safety glass
   c. an easily adjustable strap that locks in place
   d. a suitable nosepiece, which enables you to equalize the air pressure in your ears and sinuses by squeezing your nostrils shut and making your ears 'pop'
   e. the mask should give a reasonably wide field of vision and shouldn't have much depth, resulting in a low volume of air, which helps snorkellers to equalize pressure, prevent mask squeeze and facilitate the clearing of water from the mask when submersed
3. Scour the inside of a new mask's face plate with an abrasive detergent or toothpaste. This technique will help keep the glass from fogging up.
4. Before entering the water, spit on the inside of the glass and rub it briskly with your fingers; then rinse the mask in seawater. Once again, this helps to prevent fogging.
5. If your mask is a good fit, it is unnecessary to over-tighten the strap. An uncomfortably tight mask can produce headaches and any mask leakage is more likely caused by strands of hair caught under the mask, so always be sure that your hair, hood or bathing cap are not under the edge of your mask or you will be forever surfacing to empty it.

Snorkels

The two main considerations when buying a snorkel are comfort and breathing resistance. Choose a snorkel with a comfortable mouthpiece and a bore of approximately two centimetres. Thinner snorkels are difficult to breathe through and wider types can be difficult to clear of water. Avoid snorkels with sharply angled bends or concertina-type tubes: these create breathing resistance and trap water. A valve in the bend of a snorkel can help with water clearance but will always be a point of weakness that can trap sand and cause leakages, thus reducing its life expectancy.

The flange on the snorkel's mouthpiece is secured between teeth and lips, and the projections sit behind the teeth. When selecting your snorkel, try breathing through it slowly and evenly before you enter the sea for the first time.

Some underwater explorers choose to snorkel to avoid the encumberance of dive gear.

Always remember to hold the snorkel firmly with your lips, which will create a pouting expression that improves the mask's seal on your face. Never grimace, as this deepens the furrows above your mouth and allows water to leak in. One short sharp exhalation through the snorkel is usually enough to blow out any water, although beginners may find it easier to lift their heads out of the water, remove the snorkel and tip it upside down. This is laborious and clumsy, so it is worth mastering the proper technique for removing water.

While floating on the surface you should always look slightly ahead. This will keep your snorkel pointing upwards. If you look directly downwards, the snorkel will be angled forwards and its opening will come closer to the water's surface, allowing water to flood in.

When you take the plunge and free-dive underwater, the snorkel will fill up, but your mouth will not be flooded. To clear this water, look up as you ascend and blow out when your mask breaks the surface. It is easier to clear the snorkel while it points down than to blow the water upwards. If you do not have enough air left to blow the water out, you will have to remove the mouthpiece upon surfacing.

Fins

You have a choice between full-foot and open-heel fins. Full-foot fins are lighter and less hard on the ankles for people who like to swim long distances. Also, because boots are not a prerequisite, they allow you to cut back on the amount of gear you need to buy, pack, carry and clean. Open-heel fins have an adjustable strap for a perfect fit.

A mask, snorkel and fins – all you need to enjoy Oman's mysterious underwater world.

However, they are bulky and must be worn with a pair of underwater boots.

Whatever style you prefer, make sure the blades are rigid; this allows for more propulsion with each kick.

Keep your fins underwater (sometimes a problem with floating types). Fins flapping at the surface offer virtually no propulsion and terrify the fish. Kick your legs up and down, bending more at the knee than at the waist. Do not cycle, ie drawing the knees up to the waist.

Your snorkelling technique will quickly improve with a little practice – just work on relaxing, moving slowly and enjoying yourself. You may need to smooth your duck dive (your dive from the surface downwards) as quick, jerky movements waste energy and chase away fish and turtles.

To dive down, bend at the waist, pull your legs up to your chest, raise them out of the water, then simply relax and let gravity do the work.

Once your fins are underwater, you can slowly begin to fin your way further down. Move sparingly and you will find your breath lasts longer. To avoid painful pressure on the eardrums, you need to equalize and should begin to 'pop' your ears at the surface, and continue all the way down. Moving your jaw from side to side or opening your mouth wide and yawning can work as well; otherwise simply hold your nose between thumb and forefinger and blow slowly but forcefully through the nose.

Once you are proficient at snorkelling, you may be lured by scuba diving. It is always best to learn to dive from a certified instructor, as you may not be permitted to dive by any dive operators without evidence of your qualifications.

With comfortable gear and good company, scuba diving can be a fascinating experience.

Commercial Dive Operators

Muscat

BluZone Watersports

Accredited both as a PADI Gold Palm Resort and as a BSAC Resort, BluZone Watersports has all the facilities, equipment and resources to offer instruction and certification through various PADI levels, diving/ snorkelling excursions and rental or purchase of a wide range of equipment. Its location, at Marina Bandar ar Rawdah, ensures the convenience of wet-berthed dive boats and quick access to Muscat's dive sites. Qualified PADI Divemasters or Instructors lead every dive. A complete itinerary for visiting divers can be arranged, including accom-modation at any of the nearby hotels.

Tel: +968 24737293
Email: Bluzone@omantel.net.om
Website: www.bluzonediving.com

DivEco

DivEco runs dive operations at the Al Sawadi Beach Resort, which is run from the appropriately named Daymaniyat Dive Centre and specialises in dive trips to the nearby Daymaniyat Islands. Instruction and PADI certification are offered at both locations and a full range of rental equipment is also available. Excursions leave from the beach immediately outside the resort. Like most dive operators in Muscat, DivEco also offers snorkelling and dolphin-watching trips.

Tel: +968 26795545
Email: diveco@hotmail.com
Website: www.alsawadibeach.com

Moon Light Dive Centre (Hyatt Regency Hotel)

Moon Light Dive Centre, situated on the beach in The Boat House, currently runs diving operations at the Hyatt Regency Hotel. Dive excursions cater for hotel guests and the general public and many other water-sports activities are also on offer. Both diving and snorkelling equipment is available for hire. A complete range of PADI courses are offered in both English and Arabic.

Tel: +968 99317700
Email: aljoori@omantel.net.om
Website: www.moonlightdive.com

Muscat Diving and Adventure Centre

For dive trips in the Muscat area, Muscat Diving and Adventure Centre (MDAC) will refer you to the BluZone Watersports centre (see left). However, trips to more remote dive sites are also catered for, using 4WD vehicles to access shore-diving locations, usually involving overnight camps. Other activities can be arranged for the non-diving partner or family. A complete range of rental equipment is available for diving and snorkelling.

Tel: +968 24485663
Email: info@omandiving.com
Website: www.omandiving.com

Oman Dive Centre

The Oman Dive Centre (ODC) was formerly operated under the auspices of the Oman Diving Federation (now dis-banded) and is currently under the management of the Al Bustan Palace Hotel. The ODC is situated in Bandar Jissah, one of Oman's most beautiful and rich natural heritage sites. The centre

Most dive stores and opertators in Oman can outfit you from head to toe.

offers a complete range of PADI diving courses, in both English and Arabic, and is well equipped. Dive excursions, led by qualified PADI Divemasters or Instructors, are offered throughout the capital and beach cabanas are available for overnight stays at the centre.

Tel: +968 24824240
Email: info@omandivecentre.com
Website: www.diveoman.com.om

THE MUSANDAM PENINSULA

Al Marsa Travel and Tourism

Established in 2000, Al Marsa Travel and Tourism offers dive excursions on board dhows or speedboats from Dibba in southern Musandam. Day cruises or weeklong live-aboard trips mostly target dive sites around the Musandam Peninsula, although trips can span as far afield as the Daymaniyat Islands. PADI-qualified staff lead the trips.

Tel: +968 26836550 (Oman);
     +971 65441232 (UAE)
Email: info@musandamdiving.com
Website: www.musandamdiving.com

Charlotte Anne Sailing and Diving Charters

Charters aboard the *Charlotte Anne*, a twin-mast schooner accommodating up to 11 guests, can be arranged directly with Charlotte Anne Sailing and Diving Charters based in Fujairah. The vessel operates mainly in the Musandam region, offering day trips and longer excursions. Live-aboard cruises to other parts of Oman can be arranged on request as can diving equipment upon 72 hours notice, although you are requested to bring your own snorkelling gear.

Tel: +971 9 2223508 (UAE)
Email: seatrips@emirates.net.ae (UAE)
Website: www.charlotteannecharters.com

Khasab Travel and Tours

Trips to dive sites in the Musandam region are offered by Khasab Travel and Tours onboard a traditional dhow departing from Khasab Port. Accommodation in Khasab can be arranged and overnight camping excursions are also offered, including a guide to help identify dive sites. Dive cylinders, weights and snorkelling gear can be rented on request.

Tel: +968 26730464 (Oman);
     +971 42669950 (UAE)
Email: khastour@omantel.net.om
Website: www.khasabtours.com

SALALAH

Sumahram Falcon Watersports & Diving Centre

The most established dive centre in Salalah, Sumahram has two offices; one operates from the Crowne Plaza Hotel (formerly the Holiday Inn) and the other from the Hilton Hotel. Experienced dive leaders with excellent local knowledge of dive sites and sea conditions offer friendly and professional services. Full dive gear can be hired upon request and both shore and boat dives are available.

Tel: Hilton +968 23211234/99099002
    Crowne Plaza +968 23235427
Email: sumahram@hotmail.com

Dive Watersports Centre

The only other commercial dive operator in Dhofar, the Dive Watersports Centre in Salalah offers shore dives along the rocky coast in the Marbat region. Transport is provided by road from Salalah to the dive site, ideal for exploring the underwtarer landscape. Dive/snorkelling gear is available for hire and a local dive guide can be arranged upon request.

Tel: +968 95205750
Website: www.salalahtour.com

Dive Clubs

There are currently two BSAC dive clubs in the Muscat area and each offer membership to the general public: the Capital Area Yacht Centre (CAYC) Dive Club, and Muscat Divers, based at Marina Bandar ar Rawdah. Training is offered and newcomers are loaned equipment if required. Informal dive trips, sometimes to remote areas, are often arranged at weekends. BSAC clubs in Oman ask a nominal membership fee and are self-sufficient, with equipment servicing and maintenance performed within the club.

Other BSAC clubs in Oman have more restricted membership, such as at the Ras al Hamra Recreation Centre,

with membership restricted to PDO (Petroleum Development Oman) personnel, and at Thumrayt (Dhofar), where membership is limited to Airworks' employees. The level of activity largely depends on the members involved, so it is worth asking around to find out each club's status and activities. BSAC Dive Clubs:
Marina Bandar ar Rawdah: +968 24737296
CAYC: +968 24737712

Areas with restricted access

Access to the Daymaniyat Islands is by permit only as the islands and surrounding waters make up a nature reserve. Permits for diving in the reserve are provided upon request to the Ministry of Environment and Climate Affairs (MECA), Directorate General of Nature Conservation. The Royal Oman Police (ROP) Coastguard Operations also needs to be notified of your intended visit. Landing on the islands from May 1–October 31 is not permitted.

A permit is also required from the MECA before camping at Ras al Hadd. Do not expect to camp on the beach

The right equipment will lead to greater enjoyment during your dive experience.

and do not drive on the turtle beaches to launch your boat.

Permission is required from the ROP Coastguard before diving at Fahl Island near Muscat and around Raysut Rock near Salalah.

Diving is prohibited, by order of the ROP, at the wrecks off Al Qurm Beach and As Seeb Airport Beach, and anywhere between Sidab and Ras al Hamra. Snorkelling is apparently tolerated at Kalbuh and Cemetery Bay. However, regulations on diving and snorkelling in Oman, currently governed by the ROP Coastguard and the MECA, are subject to change. It is advisable to seek the latest information from one of the dive clubs/tour operators.

Prohibited activities

The Ministry of Agriculture and Fisheries has issued a number of laws controlling the capture, collection and export of marine life, and snorkellers and divers should abide by them:

- The collection and/or export of corals, sea shells and other marine life, whether for personal or commercial reasons, is totally prohibited. Abide by the law.
- The use of spear guns is strictly forbidden and a permit is required for fishing with a hook and line. The capture of lobsters (crayfish) and abalone is also prohibited.

Dive-operator rules

Most dive operators in Oman have their own set of rules, which include government regulations as well as strict codes of conduct. In general, divers are urged not to touch or interfere with marine life (gloves are discouraged for this reason) and those with cameras are reminded to control their buoyancy when over coral reefs. In addition, Muslim customs dictate certain dress codes when in public places so you'll feel more comfortable dressed in a wetsuit than in a two-piece swimming costume, in the case of female snorkellers and divers.

As Oman is still a relatively new diving destination, divers should take care to ensure the highest standards are maintained so that they do not bring the sport into disrepute and continue to be well received by local residents. Flouting the rules is frowned upon.

Make sure your dive cylinder has been date-stamped when you have it serviced.

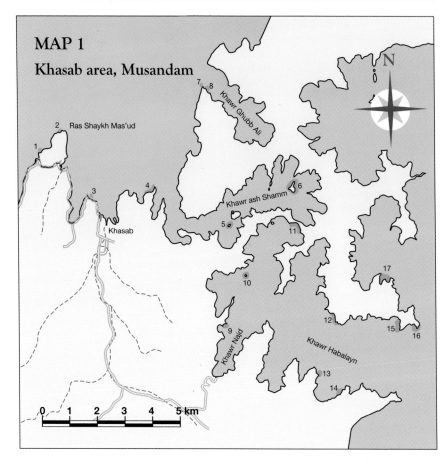

MAP 1

Khasab area, Musandam

The Musandam Peninsula

Location: Drive or fly to Khasab, base yourself at one of the hostels or hotels and contact one of the tour operators listed earlier. Alternatively, you can camp at Khawr Najd and use your own boat (or rent a small dhow or fishing boat) to explore the reefs of Khawr Habalayn (Map 1).

To dive the east coast, contact one of the operators at Daba. Alternatively, camp at the north end of the beach at Daba and rent a small dhow or fishing boat, which will take you round for the

day. Another option is to arrange for a boat to drop you off for a number of days on a good camping beach – but negotiate payment for when you get back! (Map 2)

Depth range: 1–12 metres to the base of coral reefs and inside bays, reaching 40+ metres round offshore islands.

Season: All-year-round in sheltered bays, but extremely hot in summer.

Description and special features: It is beyond the ability of any one person to

The tapering spires of the boulder coral are unique to the Musandam Peninsula.

explore all the underwater options on offer in the Musandam. Its mountainous 650-kilometre coastline is almost entirely strewn with rocks and coves. Musandam's bays, fjords and islands offer innumerable opportunities for underwater exploration. Gradual steps, increasingly steep rocky slopes and cliffs that plunge to great depths border the length of Musandam's coast.

Although coral is not quite as varied as in the Muscat area, it is more abundant and reef development is more substantial than elsewhere along the Sultanate's coast. There are large, solid reefs of a dramatic castellated boulder coral covered by tapering spires and numerous patches of cauliflower, pore and leaf corals. A type of staghorn coral forms vast tangled thickets, particularly in Khawr ash Shamm on the west coast, and tube coral forms large tree-like structures, sometimes in very shallow water where the current runs strong.

The well-shaded and sheer nature of much of the Musandam Coast favours the growth of a mix of flattened sheets of porous lettuce, flat lettuce and hedgehog corals. While the leathery and grey-green soft corals are inexplicably sparse along the bulk of the coast, the brilliant red, orange, yellow or mauve teddy-bear corals, purple and bushy orange corals, and bright yellow 'black corals' are notably abundant.

Some of the offshore rocks and islands (notably Jazirat Limah) offer spectacular diving with cliffs, caves, ledges and overhangs carpeted by a rich and colourful variety of corals and other marine life, which are swarming with shoals of fish. Schools of coachmen, yellow-bar angelfish, fusiliers, jacks and batfish, and black-tip reef sharks are a common sight. You may also be lucky to see zebra and grey reef sharks.

Also abundant, unfortunately, are huge crown-of-thorns starfish that have wreaked havoc on many coral communities of the east and north coasts.

An example of the coral variation found within Musandam's waters.

Orange Cup Corals, found on reef ledges, extend their tentacles at night in order to feed.

Ras Shaykh Mas'ud has small but scenic coral gardens in the coves along the west coast (Map 1, Sites 1 & 2). Each cove has an exclusive beach, offering a convenient base for a picnic and leisurely snorkelling or shallow diving. As access is by boat only, arrangements have to be made at Khasab (or the closer villages of Hanah, Mukhi or Qada) to have a boat both deliver and retrieve you.

Ras Salti Ali offers a convenient beach with sun shelters and water, and is a pleasant place to cool down while fish watching along the left rocky shore (Map 1, Site 3). Swim out towards the point where there are large rock boulders with caves, arches and overhangs stocked full of fish. This is the only west-coast site accessible without a boat.

Hayoot (Long Beach), south-east of Ras Shaykh Mas'ud, has a fine white sandy beach and is an excellent place for a picnic or overnight stay (Map 1, Site 4). There are sun shelters, a water tank and

a strip of coral that runs parallel to the shore. This reef is two to four-metres deep and offers pleasant snorkelling.

Khawr ash Shamm is an extremely scenic fjord with impressive rock massifs and unusually fragile coral growth (Map 1). Boulder coral, a form of leaf coral with particularly long and delicate blades, and bush, table and staghorn corals dominate the coral communities around the islands and in the more sheltered parts of the bay. There are good opportunities for snorkelling, diving and photography around Jazirat Maqlab (Telegraph Island) (Site 5) and Jazirat Sibi (Site 6), where the shallow clusters of coral on sand provide safe and easy snorkelling for beginners. There are many good sites to snorkel and dive in Khawr ash Shamm, so take the time to explore and you will most certainly be rewarded.

Khawr Ghubb Ali is a large shallow bay with unusual coral patches scattered along its coast (Map 1). There is a good dive to a depth of 25 metres down a

The tangled branches of the staghorn coral provide sanctuary for small reef fishes.

Boulder corals grow extremely slowly; these large colonies have been developing undisturbed for upwards of 200 to 300 years.

rock fall off the southern point at the entrance of the bay, where huge rock blocks attract clouds of fish (Site 7). Explore a little further into the bay along the south shore and you will find a scenic reef of boulder coral leading to large rock outcrops, offering good snorkelling and diving to depths of between 10–12 metres (Site 8).

Khawr Najd is fringed by rock with scattered corals, but one site stands out as especially interesting (Map 1, Site 9). There is dense coral growth east of the low point leading from a band of lesser brain coral over an area of mixed coral to a slope dominated almost exclusively by leaf coral. The adjacent rocky walls and ledges below the rocky point are coral-encrusted and attract a variety of

The lesser brain coral is one of the most widely spread corals in the seas of Oman.

fish. Although you can drive to the head of Khawr Najd (and this is worth doing for the view alone), a boat is needed to reach the better snorkelling sites here and in Khawr Habalayn.

Jazirat Habalayn (Map 1, Site 10) is surrounded by a truly impressive coral reef that reaches its maximum extent off the north-west corner. It is dominated by huge boulder corals, several of which must be at least 400 years old judging by their size. Unfortunately, the vast fields of bush and table corals covering the shelf that extends off the southern side of the island are now mostly dead, victims of an invasion of the harmful crown-of-thorns starfish.

Khawr Habalayn offers a variety of snorkelling and diving opportunities along its embayed, scenic coast (Map 1).

The following general description may help guide your explorations: the inner northern bays are fringed by rocks with a cover of scattered corals, principally made up of the lesser brain coral in the shallows or luxuriant patches of bush or leaf coral, and banks of cauliflower coral. For those interested in hiking up

Scuba divers peer into the awe-inspiring underwater world of the Sultanate.

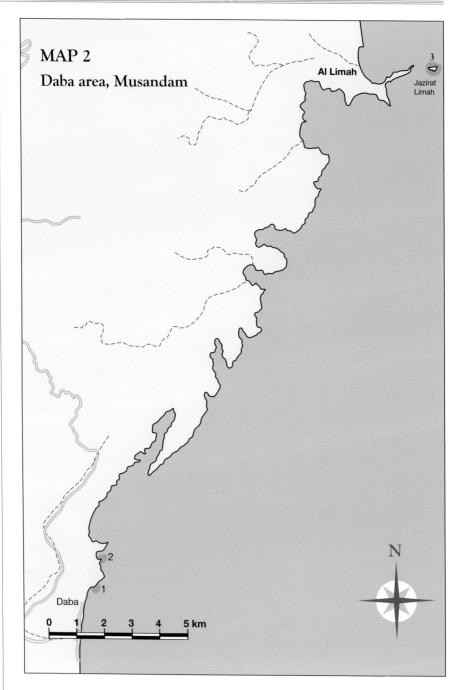

MAP 2
Daba area, Musandam

Al Limah

3

Jazirat
Limah

N

2

1

Daba

0   1   2   3   4   5 km

the saddle at Maksar to enjoy spectacular views of both Khawr ash Shamm and Khawr Habalayn, a cool dive or snorkel on your return is both refreshing and rewarding (Site 11). Corals proliferate on the rocky shelves below the steep wadis, especially in the central portion where solid reefs of boulder coral shelter hordes of fish (for example, Sites 14 & 15). The outer portions of the bays and many headlands have cliffs that drop steeply into the sea and continue underwater to great depths as walls, narrow ledges and overhangs, which are spread with sheets of encrusting corals

Snorkelling off the beach along Daba's rocky coast.

(for example, visit Sites 12 & 13). Venture out to Ras Dillah for wall diving (Site 16), or round the corner to see the beautiful reef formations in the twin bays on the northern side (Site 17).

Daba's north end has a beautiful beach with a superb campsite below the dunes and beside the ruins of stone houses. There is good snorkelling over coral gardens out around the point at the northern end of the beach (Map 2, Site 1). This is the only east-coast site accessible without a boat.

White Beach is an exquisite, small, white-sand beach backed by a bowl of steep mountains. There is excellent snorkelling out from the southern side of the beach over tiers of large table coral and a shallow dive to 12 metres off

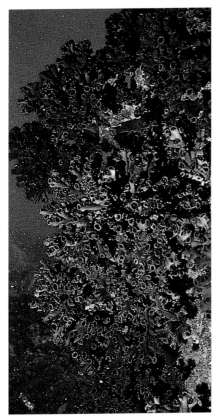

Tube corals form large trees in the strong currents of Musandam's shallower waters.

Caution: Beware of strong currents almost everywhere in the Musandam Peninsula, although a little forward planning can put them to good advantage. Also watch out for the long-spined sea urchin.

Bottlenose dolphins are known to accompany divers during their underwater excursions, emitting high-pitched calls which you may detect if you listen carefully.

More accomplished snorkellers are able to dive deep for short periods of time.

the point (Map 2, Site 2). The sheer rocks, caves and gullies at the point are a magnet for fish, such as fusiliers and some large barracuda.

Jazirat Limah (Limah Rock) is well worth a visit for the more adventurous (Map 2, Site 3). Travel up by dhow and enjoy the stunning mountain scenery en route. The shores of the island are steep-sided and, underwater, a series of ledges and overhangs are carpeted with colourful soft corals, purple coral (which appears bright blue underwater), large trees of tube coral, yellow bushes of 'black coral' and teddy bear corals in an array of red and orange hues. You are bound to see bigger fish and black-tip reef sharks here. This is a good place for a drift dive, but be very careful of the strong tidal currents.

Caution: The strong currents in this region are excellent for drift dives.

Close-up of a scorpionfish which has poisonous spines along its back that it erects when in a defensive posture.

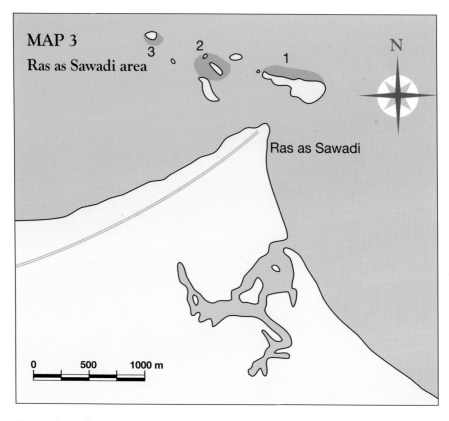

MAP 3
Ras as Sawadi area

N

Ras as Sawadi

0   500   1000 m

Ras as Sawadi

Location: Ras as Sawadi located on the Al Batinah Coast between Barka and Wudam, is approximately 80 kilometres from Al Qurm past As Seeb. Turn off at the signpost and follow the tarmac road to a parking lot beside the beach (Map 3). The Daymaniyat Dive Centre is located at the Al Sawadi Beach Resort.

Depth range: 1–12 metres.

Caution: Strong currents that sweep through the islands make diving both dangerous and exciting.

Season: All-year-round, but winter winds may stir up silt, reducing visibility to less than one metre.

Description and special features: Ras as Sawadi is a scenic sandy point strewn with shells at its tidemark. Seven islands lie close to the mainland, the largest of which can be reached on foot across a shallow sand bar.

It is possible to snorkel along the rocky shores of the main island and the northern side offers a shallow dive over rocky substrate (Site 1). The snorkelling is better in the sheltered waters around the central group of four small islands, where there are many coral colonies and some small patches of reef (Site 2).

Pincushion starfishes are conspicuous members of Oman's reef communities.

The southern side of the western-most island has the most extensive and continuous coral cover. This colourful reef is formed from banks of cauliflower, bush, table and hood corals, and is frequently carpeted by vast schools of snappers. Other reef fish such as fusiliers, which shoal in great numbers in mid water, are in abundance too. The sea is generally clearer here than around the other islands (Site 3).

Daymaniyat Islands

Location: The string of nine main islands with numerous rock satellites, reefs and shoals (areas of shallow water), lie approximately 18 kilometres off the Al Batinah Coast from As Seeb to Barka, stretching for 20 kilometres in an east-west direction (Maps 4, 5 & 6).

Depth range: 1–30 metres.

Season: Visitors are not permitted to land on the islands between the beginning of May until the end of October. The area can be rough during the winter months, particularly in February, March and April.

Description and special features: Except for the easternmost island, which rests on a shoal, the islands' north faces tend to have cliffs and, from here, the islands slope southwards toward the sea. These cliffs continue below water as sheer

Corals attract different species of fishes who use their snouts to find food within crevices.

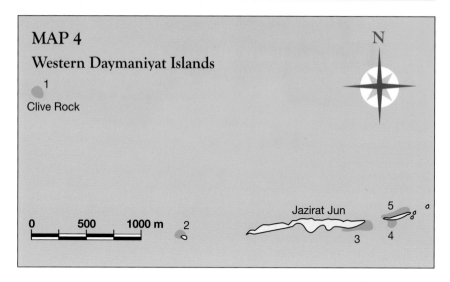

MAP 4

Western Daymaniyat Islands

N

1
Clive Rock

0   500   1000 m   2

Jazirat Jun   5

3   4

drops or steep slopes of tumbled rock to depths of 20–25 metres. Wide shallow shelves of sand and coral, with occasional coral-bound rocky outcrops, border the southern parts of the islands.

Patch and fringing reefs of bush, table, pore and boulder corals are well developed along the sheltered southern sides of the islands. Unfortunately, many of the reefs are now dead, apparently the victims of attack by coral-eating crown-of-thorns starfish along with the periodic upwelling of cold seawater.

The islands offer a variety of habitats for coral settlement, including under-

The Arabian butterflyfish is a colourful member of the Sultanate's coral reefs.

water cliffs, ledges and overhangs, and shallow rocky shelves and outcrops in both exposed and sheltered locations. Consequently, the diversity of corals and other bottom-dwelling creatures is relatively high, as are dive options.

Bottlenose, spinner and long-beaked common dolphins (the latter two sometimes travel in mixed schools of several hundred), and an occasional whale shark, increase the chances of a different dive for the adventurous. Humpback whales have been seen close to the islands on a number of occasions, offering a rare and exciting experience both above and below the water.

Jazirat Jun (Map 4), the westernmost island, is 19 kilometres north-east of Ras as Sawadi, and 27 kilometres north-west of As Seeb. The wide beautiful beach on the south side of the island makes an ideal base for exploring both the immediate island area and the offshore reefs. A large shoal lies about two kilometres north-west of Jun (Site 1) and a smaller shoal with an emerging rock lies about 500 metres west of the

The humpback dolphin is seen quite often in Oman's seas and will add an element of fun to your underwater experience.

island (Site 2). Both offer good wall-diving opportunities down their northern flanks to depths of between 20–25 metres, as well as in narrow gullies. The larger of the two has extensive banks of coral, especially along the northern edge, and many more fish. Its shallowest point is approximately eight-metres deep.

There is a remarkable starburst coral patch – 400-square metres wide and one-metre thick – about one kilometre south of the beach on Jazirat Jun.

There are excellent snorkelling and shallow-diving opportunities along the south-east point of the island (Site 3). The rocky shore here is fringed by a narrow reef platform that spreads out over a scenic reef of boulder coral that attracts and shelters vast numbers of

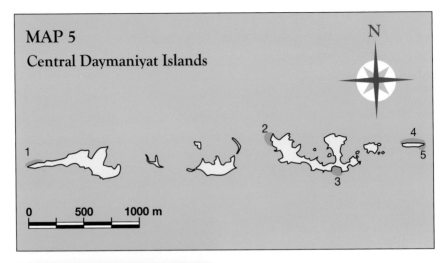

MAP 5

Central Daymaniyat Islands

N

0   500   1000 m

A zebra shark, decorated by a pair of remoras, lies on a bed of bean coral.

fish, most notably Sohal surgeonfish in great profusion. If the current is not too strong through the cut between Jun and its eastern neighbour, it's possible to swim south from the end of the boulder-coral reef over the banks of cauliflower coral. Their bright purples, the many anemones occupied by clownfish and the shoals of coachmen and other fish make for a rewarding foray.

A truly splendid boulder-coral reef, some colonies knobbed and others smooth, borders the Jun side of its

neighbouring rocky islet to the east (Site 4). The northern side of this islet offers a sheer drop of between 20–25 metres making for a good drift dive or snorkel when the current is strong (Site 5). Barracudas constantly patrol this drop-off, as well as the channel edge of the boulder-coral reef.

The central islands offer a great variety of snorkelling and diving opportunities (Map 5). For the snorkellers there are many shallow patches of bush, table, cauliflower and boulder corals scattered close to the beaches, and the tumbled-rock reefs and walls below the northern cliffs invite exploration by divers. For example, the north-western areas of the main and westernmost islands offer good dive sites (Sites 1 & 2) and a drift dive along the north face and back up the southern side of the easternmost island is spectacular (Sites 4 & 5).

Caution: Beware of the currents in some of the more exposed locations and please ensure that you have adequate surface boat support.

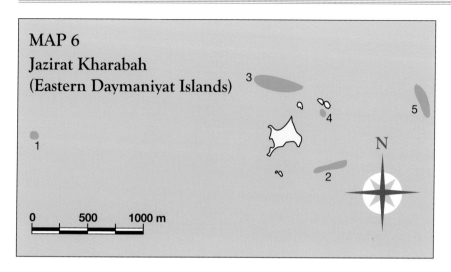

MAP 6
Jazirat Kharabah
(Eastern Daymaniyat Islands)

Turtle encounters are common here and sheer rock walls and ledges that continue to depths of between 22–27 metres teem with life, such as sponges, seasquirts, teddy bear corals, basketstars and a type of black coral with extended bright-yellow tentacles.

The bay east of the guardhouse on the south side of the island (Site 3) stands alone for coral abundance, development and scenery. Huge boulder corals cover much of the bay, forming a reef of varying contours cut by narrow gullies. A shallow rock terrace on the east side of the bay has a colourful garden of bush, hood and cauliflower corals.

Jazirat Kharabah (Map 6), the eastern island, lies 17 kilometres north of As Seeb and 39 kilometres north-west of Ras al Hamra. This exquisite island is ringed by beaches and offers many snorkelling and diving options. The shallow waters close to shore harbour many patches of coral and abundant fish and are ideally suited for the more shore-bound snorkeller. There are rocky and coral reefs in every direction off the island. Banks of cauliflower coral with large schools of parrotfish can be found off the southern side (Site 2). An attractive boulder-coral reef stretches across the northern side in 6–13 metres of water (Site 3) and a smaller, shallower reef thrives in the shelter of the rocky islet east of Kharabah (Site 4).

Rocky outcrops and coral patches are scattered over the shoal, which extends

A cabbage coral mingles alongside nestled in a bed of brown seaweed.

Caution: As always when in a conservation area, take special care not to damage or disturb any reef life. This is a regionally significant site for nesting hawksbill turtles.

The long spires of this boulder coral give it a castellated appearance that is not commonly seen in Oman.

Cauliflower coral colonizes quickly and tends to grow in disturbed areas.

for a considerable distance east of Kharabah. The eastern edge of the shoal is rimmed by a rocky ridge, which is carpeted with leathery, soft corals and scored with deep, sandy gullies, that drop sharply from seven to 20 metres (Site 5).

To the west of Jazirat Kharabah is a large rocky shoal, which is great for diving when not festooned with fishing

Nestled among a forest of pink teddy bear coral is a single patch of orange cup coral.

nets and traps. The shoal is between 12–15 metres in depth, with a sheer drop to more than 25 metres deep along the south-western side, and it has a shallow rocky outcrop that reaches between four and five-metres deep. Coral growth here is good: there are well developed patches of boulder coral forming mazes of tunnels and gullies in which large moray eels, many kinds of reef fish, large groupers and turtles are

found, while one school of blue-line snappers found here is believed to consist of some 10,000 fish (Site 1).

The islands are an important conservation area for coral communities, the highly endangered hawksbill turtle that nests from March to June, and for nesting green turtles and seabirds during the summer months. At the moment there are no restrictions on diving around the islands, other than laws that prohibit access during the closed season, and those that prevent spear fishing, the collection of coral and sea shells and the capture of spiny lobsters. Please adhere to these rules and make every effort to avoid damaging the reefs while anchoring or diving.

For those camping here overnight during March and April, before the islands are closed to visitors, please make sure you extinguish your lanterns by 8.30 pm to avoid interfering with nesting hawksbill turtles.

Caution: Rocks in the intertidal area can be extremely slippery, so take care when entering or leaving the sea. Keep well clear of the illegal spear fishermen that frequent this area and be careful when you are in murky conditions.

Marjan Public Beach

Location: North coast of Ras al Hamra, west of the Ras al Hamra Recreation Centre. Public parking is available across from the beach (Map 7, Site 2).

Depth range: Coral immediately offshore lies between one and three metres below sea level, reaching six to seven metres off rocky headlands.

Season: All-year-round, although it is frequently rough during the winter months, particularly between December and February.

Description and special features: Marjan Public Beach is one of the few good snorkelling sites accessible to the public from land and it is an ideal spot for beginners. The bay is very safe and the water is often calm and clear. Numerous

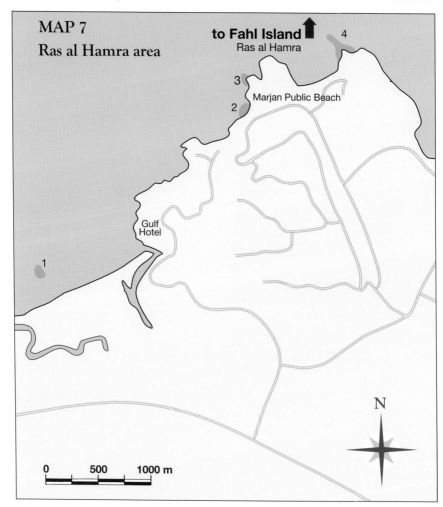

MAP 7
Ras al Hamra area

to Fahl Island
Ras al Hamra
4

3

Marjan Public Beach
2

Gulf Hotel

1

N

0   500   1000 m

School of fusiliers dazzle snorkellers in Oman's waters, adding to their excitement.

patches of boulder and lesser brain corals, surrounded by a host of colourful fish, lie scattered on sand in shallow

Fishes throng around the large flat rock off Marjan Public Beach.

waters towards the eastern side of the bay. Beginners can choose a comfortable depth from literally standing on the sand beside a coral head to floating in deeper water along the edge of shallow corals, without fear of being scratched. Later, when your confidence and ability increase, you may like to drift over the reef and look for cuttlefish among the profusion of fish and other reef creatures. From time to time a turtle will take up temporary residence in the bay, thrilling snorkellers with its proximity as it becomes less afraid of them.

Towards the point on the eastern headland, a large flat rock lies just off

The whale shark – gentle giant of the seas.

the cliff (Site 2) (be careful not to confuse this with the small pointed rock closer to the beach). The base of this rock contains a small tunnel, which is crowded with fish. The cliff face opposite is riddled with small tunnels, caves and crevices packed with fish, which are excellent for exploring and, at times, hundreds of fish have been known to carpet the seabed.

On a calm day it is worth continuing along the coastline around Ras al Hamra, although the swim may be a little ambitious for most beginners (especially if they have to swim back as well). The eroded cliff faces and fallen rocks harbour a variety of life, including sponges and sea ferns, and turtles are regularly seen in the area. A small beach at the head of a sandy bay harbouring corals similar to those off Marjan Beach lies a short way beyond Site 3 – a good place to haul out and rest or warm up.

Shark Point

Location: Shark Point is the headland dividing the Ras al Hamra Recreation Centre (RHRC) of PDO and the oil refinery beach. This area is best reached by boat, although it is not too far a swim from the RHRC Beach and there is plenty to see on the way (Map 7, Site 4).

Depth range: 1–6 metres.

Season: All-year-round, but the sea can get rough during the winter, particularly in January, February and March.

Description and special features: There are some interesting rock formations, both above and below the surface of the water, which run along the western ridge of the headland and terminate at the point. Particularly interesting for snorkellers is the series of shallow caves and tunnels, which are crowded with

The nurse shark is sluggish and not considered dangerous but should never be provoked.

cave-dwelling fish. Some of these caves penetrate deep into the cliff wall and the rock can be sharp, so be careful.

An area consisting of mostly lesser brain coral spreads out from the base of the cliff and is interspersed with starry cup, spine and other corals. Further out, an area of ridges and ledges covered by soft corals, sponges and scattered coral

A black-tip reef shark patrols a low-lying coral bed in search of its next meal.

colonies can be found; corals protected by small coves and valleys between the finger-like spurs of rock that project out from the cliff have flourished and so are of a considerable size.

The seabed then drops several times and each large platform of rock stretches out towards Fahl Island. Corals and fish become sparser as the water gets deeper, but what does become evident is the large fleshy artichoke coral, unique to Oman. There are very few examples of this coral in the Sultanate and the main population of this rare animal is centred here. So please be especially careful with anchors or diving and don't even consider collecting samples.

> Caution: A number of large sharks have been seen in this area, so it is advisable not to swim here.

The Sohal surgeonfish is a photogenic resident of the Sultanate's coral and rocky reefs.

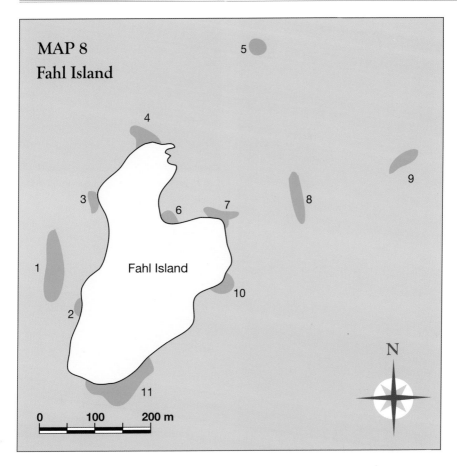

MAP 8
Fahl Island

Fahl Island

Fahl Island

Location: Four kilometres north of Ras al
Hamra; access is by boat only (Map 8).

Depth range: 3–42 metres.

Season: All-year-round, but it can be
rough during the winter months. ROP
permission is required for diving.

Description and special features: There
are a large number of excellent diving
and snorkelling sites around Fahl Island
so, unless the sea is very rough, you will

generally find calm waters and good
dives. In addition, as the island lies well
offshore, the sea is often clearer here
than along the mainland coastline.

The area around Fahl Island has the
greatest variety of corals ever discovered
in the Sultanate, including four corals
yet to be found elsewhere in Oman, and
seven nowhere else in the Muscat area.

Caution: Strong currents sweep round
the island. So plan your dives carefully
at the deeper sites, especially in the
northern and southern sectors.

Caves and tunnels attract fishes for the food and protection they provide within.

This is a valuable conservation area, so please take especially good care to avoid damaging the coral while anchoring or diving and resist the urge to collect.

The entire western side of the island is a great area to snorkel or dive (Site 1). There is a rocky shelf, averaging about 10–12-metres deep, with numerous but fairly small coral colonies, sandy gullies and large numbers of fish. Some extremely large moray eels can be seen here, along with numerous, rather aggressive triggerfish. About 100 metres offshore the shelf drops down a coral-encrusted wall for around 20–22 metres. Although parts of this western shelf are quite barren, sea life abounds on the many rocky outcrops and coral patches.

The entrance to the Large Western Tunnel is concealed behind a cluster of large rocks in a small cove (Site 2). Although relatively devoid of life, this tunnel is an interesting formation to explore. Upon entry, it slopes down slightly for about 40 metres before hitting a t-junction. At this point, it is too narrow for more than a single diver. So far as we know, no one has explored to the ends of the tee. Exploring this far is somewhat risky, so it is best to follow the example of the fish and stay out

Resembling schools of sardines with which they can be easily confused, scads travel in schools that can contain many hundreds of fishes.

towards the mouth of the tunnel where the marine life is concentrated.

South Bumps, the rock cluster at the mouth of the western tunnel, provides a haven for sea life and supports many different kinds of coral, such as the red cave coral. It also provides shelter for large Malabar groupers (Site 2).

Bill's Bumps are a cluster of huge rocks separated by narrow gullies that lie below the overhanging cliff towards the north-west point of the island (Site 3). The rocks sit at a depth of around 17 metres at their deepest to between five and eight metres at their shallowest. Although the rocks are rather devoid of crustacea, they attract large numbers of fish. Snorkellers and divers will surely find this site is rewarding.

North Point or North Bumps are similar to Bill's Bumps, but often enjoy clearer water between the rocks and the island than elsewhere around the island (Site 4). Schools of snapper and small barracuda frequently circle round them, fusiliers shoal above, large jacks power among them and several sizeable Malabar groupers occupy the caves at their base. Huge rays glide gracefully past, including the occasional manta. It is here that the lucky are rewarded most often with views of whale sharks.

The black-tip reef shark is so named for its distinctive black dorsal fin.

A swim from North Point out to sea on a bearing just a few degrees west of north will ultimately lead you to a line of rocks, running in an east-west direction in about 30 metres of water. There is a small tug wreck further seaward, about 42 metres down. The rocks and tug attract large fish and are festooned with beautiful soft corals. Although the line of rocks can be combined with a dive from North Point, the tug is too far off and needs a dedicated dive.

Deep Reef is north-north-east of Fahl Island (Site 5), but you will need someone who knows the location well to take you to the site. Deep Reef is a large rocky outcrop rising from the sandy seabed at 42-metres deep to a minimum depth of some 22 metres. This is a superb deep dive for the more experienced diver. The outcrop is covered with soft and unusual deep-water corals, with many growing as flat sheets and others as small isolated cups. Cylindrical white soft corals that resemble Dead man's fingers of the North Atlantic, carpet the lower parts of the rock.

Emperor angelfish are shy but this one was most willing to pose for photographs.

North Bay or Ray Bay is a useful refuge from westerly winds and a good place to find rays (Site 6). The shallower parts of the bay have large rocks and boulder coral strewn around sandy patches where the rays can be found. Most fish seem to congregate around the massive rocks at the southern edge of the bay where they dart for cover in the numerous nooks and crannies. The bay dips gently seaward over huge sheets of coral to a sandy slope.

The wrecks of a tug and barge lie on this slope at a maximum high-tide depth of 30 and 27 metres respectively (Site 8). Swim down from the headland towards the eastern end of North Bay over stepped rock ledges and scattered rocks covered by tall purple coral to a depth of

between 18–20 metres (in fact, this area makes a good dive in its own right) (Site 7). Continue out down the sandy slope at an angle of 60 degrees until you reach the 27-metre deep contour (2–3 minutes from the headland). Turn left and look out for the tug (a further 1–2 minutes).

This small tug is a haven of life, most of which cannot be seen in shallower waters. It is a photographer's dream – a colourful collection of bushy orange and purple corals, teddy bear coral and a host of barnacles. A closer look reveals featherduster worms in yellow, red, blue and black, spiral-gill worms, banded featherstars and delicate brittlestars. Rank upon rank of unusually large cardinalfish crowd round the wheelhouse and along the deck. The fish here are clearly accustomed to

The white-spotted eagle ray is often seen digging in the sand with its snout in search of food and occasionally makes spectacular leaps from the water.

A yellow featherstar finds a convenient perch among the branches of the purple coral.

divers and quite obviously unafraid. A large Malabar grouper lives under the stern, where cleaner wrasses busy themselves removing parasites from around its head, even entering its mouth and cleaning the gills. Look out for the unusual deeper-water fish, in particular Gardiner's butterflyfish and the spotted-tail hawkfish, recognizable by its red-flecked white tail and habit of sitting motionless on the wreck.

There's a line that leads from the tug to the barge. However, it will take many dives, made all too short by the allotted dive time, before one can pass the tug by to find the barge.

The two large rocks of Shallow Reef lie east of North Bay and drop from 17–35 metres below sea level (Site 9). Sponges and a number of different hard and soft corals cover the rocky outcrops. This attractive site is made all the more enjoyable by the great quantities of fish that gather there in abundance, some massing in large schools.

East Bay, the more southern of the two small coves on the relatively uninteresting east coast, has a collection of tumbled rocks, which are fascinating to explore (Site 10). A spur of coral-encrusted rock and sand slopes gently out from the north side of this cove from three to more than 20 metres deep. Huge schools of fish often shoal over this reef, casting dark shadows on the bottom. Seaward of the reef, a large dome of rock rises slightly above the sandy seabed and supports a swaying garden of purple coral.

The East Tunnel connects East Bay to the small cove immediately north of it. The tunnel broadens from a narrow entrance in East Bay to a large cave in the cove. Huge schools of fish occasionally crowd the tunnel and make a

The Durban shrimp are night wanderers, usually found on rocky reefs and shipwrecks.

thunderous noise when disturbed. Some sizeable sharks have also been seen in the tunnel on occasion.

South Point has a small sandy beach at low tide. East of the line of rocks running out from the beach is a beautiful shallow reef formed from a rolling carpet of purple cauliflower coral, broken by an occasional patch of large boulder coral (Site 11). It is a popular snorkelling site. Black-tip reef sharks, spotted eagle rays and large oceanic triggerfish are conspicuous among the more colourful emperor angelfish, surgeonfish, parrotfish, butterflyfish and Moorish idols. The reef slopes gradually seaward to a depth of 6–8 metres, where the purple cauliflower coral eventually gives way to massed hillocks of boulder coral and an explosion of fish. Boulder corals become sparse further offshore, ending on sand at a depth of 15 metres.

Strong currents generally scour this area, particularly the rocky shelf at the extreme southern end. The rocky shore beside the cauliflower-coral reef is a lovely place to snorkel: it has varied topography including tumbled rock, arches, shelves, caves and short tunnels covered in places by hood coral in a patchwork of mauves, blue-greens, warm browns and purples, with the occasional yellow-green bush coral and purple cauliflower coral adding contrast. Also watch for the experimental artificial reef (a series of concrete 'reefballs') deployed by the Ministry of Regional Municipalities, Environment and Water Resources.

Caution: Only the best snorkellers can swim through the tunnel in one breath, but this is not advised. Divers should find the short swim exciting.

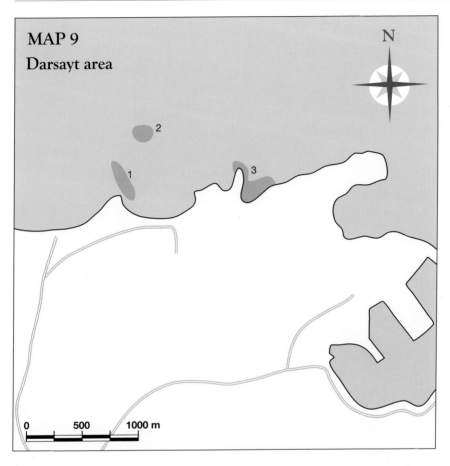

MAP 9
Darsayt area

N

0   500   1000 m

Darsayt

Location: Darsayt can be reached by road and is signposted on the Al Qurm–Ruwi highway, or by boat, situated just east of the oil refinery (Map 9).

Depth range: 2–14 metres.

Season: All-year-round, but the waters of the Darsayt area are frequently rough during the winter months. You will find this to be the case particularly in January, February and March. Snorkelling only: diving is prohibited.

Description and special features: There are a number of good snorkelling sites off the small beach east of Darsayt; the offshore rocky reef, in particular, offers unique underwater scenery.

A large rocky reef reaching depths of up to 14 metres lies about half-a-kilometre off the eastern beach (Site 2). It can often be found by the fishing nets and traps that surround it. Huge shoals of fish hover over rocky outcrops, where numerous small bush and encrusting pore corals, and large table and boulder corals have gained a foothold. The reef

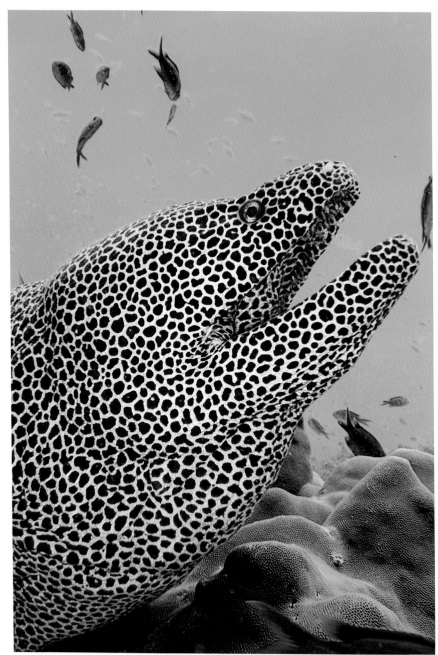

Though usually quite gentle, the honeycomb moray can inflict a nasty bite if provoked.

A crown of bright-green tentacles caps the extended polyps of this daisy coral colony.

is surrounded by some huge vase corals, the most pristine examples to be found in the Muscat area. Banks of cauliflower coral lead off the east side into the bay. Look out for large slipper lobsters nestled in the vase corals – curious brownish lobsters with a pair of flattened blade-like antennae, instead of the usual extended spiny ones.

The eastern coves to the right of the eastern beach also offer good snorkelling. The largest corals are found off the eastern shore of the second and larger cove (Site 3). There are large brain corals, equally impressive table corals, a vast field of daisy coral with swaying tentacles, dense leaf coral and a

Caution: Snorkellers should be careful of the scorpionfish lying well camouflaged on the rocky sea floor of the shallow bays.

variety of bush, hood and larger star corals covering about 85 per cent of the tumbled rock slope. Fish are abundant, particularly large parrotfish, and small schooling barracuda are often present. This area is often the calmest and clearest and has slightly deeper water (9–10 metres) than the neighbouring bays. Small black-tip reef sharks are quite a common sight in the warm shallow waters, but pose no threat to humans.

Slipper lobsters are distinguishable by their flat, rather than protruding antennae.

MAP 10
Muscat area

N

0   500   1000 m

Kalbuh

Location: Kalbuh is a small village at the end of the corniche, a few hundred metres short of Muscat. Turn off the corniche, drive through the village and park near the right side of the sandy beach, or continue on across the football field. Approximately 250 metres along a rough track (either by foot or 4x4 vehicle) you'll find a small, flat clearing beside a stony beach bordered by spurs of rock (Map 10, Site 4).

Depth range: 1–14 metres.

Season: All-year-round, but the waters are frequently rough between the months of November and March. Snorkelling only, diving is prohibited.

Description and special features: This is a truly valuable snorkelling site, being easily accessible to all by car or boat. There are two entry points into the bay;

Stingrays spend most of their time covered by a layer of sand on the sea bottom.

the first from a sandy beach below the village, close to a good parking area; and the second, at the end of the park, alongside the rocky headland. But it can be difficult to enter here, especially at low tide, as it involves clambering over intertidal rocks.

The lionfish should not be touched – if provoked, it can inject poison from its backspines.

From the sandy beach, there is a gradual slope towards the centre of the bay, banked on the right by the revetment (retaining wall), which shelters numerous lionfish and groupers. The sandy floor of the bay is pitted with craters, formed by rays while in pursuit of the crabs and molluscs buried within. The sea floor is littered with well-hidden, sand-camouflaged stingrays and slightly less inconspicuous old tyres, now home to sea urchins and moray eels.

The revetment eventually leads to a varied coral garden including a scenic variety of cauliflower, brain, daisy, leaf, star, table and bush corals, among others. This coral garden is bordered on the seaward side by a 30-metre-long underwater cliff on a rocky spur, which is encrusted by brightly coloured corals. The sandy seabed at the base of the cliff face, lying at around 10-metres deep, is strewn with patches of coral that stretch seaward to depths of 14 metres.

A swim over the coral boulders and gardens, along the cliff face and out about 40 metres, and back in and around the spur to an area of rocky coves, provides an interesting and scenic snorkel. The fish-watching is excellent and the scenic environment, a variety of colourful and fascinating marine life and clear water, create some brilliant opportunities for photographing the underwater wonderland.

The sun's glare is visible overtop thousands of schooling fish.

Cemetery Bay

Location: The bay lies between Muscat Island and Sidab and is accessible by boat or via a short, but steep, *jabal* walk from Muscat. Only snorkellers should attempt the walk.

Drive past His Majesty Sultan Qaboos's palace in the direction of Sidab and park in the large car park outside the Royal Court buildings, opposite the Rainforest Cafe. There is a mosque alongside the far north-east corner of the car park, behind which is a footpath. A short walk along this footpath will take you up the side of a small *jabal* towards a fortified wall containing a small archway, which marks the point of descent towards the bay, which, initially, is rather steep. The entire walk takes between 15 and 20 minutes and you will arrive on a small pebble beach, a great point of entry into the water (Map 10).

Depth range: 0.5–4 metres around the inner bay to nine metres further out.

Season: All-year-round. Snorkelling only, diving is prohibited.

Caution: Beware of sharp rocks, oysters, sea urchins and scorpionfish when wading out from shore. Choose your entry point carefully.

Description and special features: The rocky shores of the bay are lined with scattered coral, with two large banks of cauliflower coral in 2–3 metres of water off the northern side of the bay (Site 11).

Huge, turreted boulder corals form a small reef in the sheltered water off the stony beach on the south-east side of the bay (Site 13). These corals, which reach 4–5 metres in diameter, are hundreds of years old, making them some of the oldest surviving corals in this part of Oman. Within cannon shot of Fort Jalali, the oldest of these corals would have perhaps witnessed attempts to rout the Portuguese as the attacking ships sped overhead four centuries ago.

The eroded undercut bases of these boulder corals, and the deep gullies, caves and tunnels between them, shelter porcupinefish, groupers, batfish and clouds of red-bronze sweepers, among a host of others. Parrotfish, angelfish,

A Dhofar clownfish, as yet undescribed in scientific literature, swims over bean coral.

A Dhofar clownfish can seek camouflage with the swaying fingers of its host anemone.

SNORKELLING AND DIVING IN OMAN

Caution: Be especially wary of speed-boats and water-skiers, and watch out for the abundant long-spined sea urchins on some shallow reefs.

surgeonfish, wrasse, coachmen, Moorish idols and butterflyfish shoal in a confusion of colour around and above the coral. If you look carefully, a lone barracuda might be seen patrolling the reef edge (eight-metres deep).

In shallower waters the more delicate bush and table corals – and their branches – are home to skittish damselfish who thrive in the shelter offered by their older relatives. Black-tip reef sharks frequently patrol the area.

The rocky areas are interesting too, housing spiny lobsters (painted crayfish), shrimp, crabs, and a covering of seasquirts, colourful sponges and sheets of other minute marine creatures.

The rocky headland to the right of the bay offers many opportunities for exploration for the more accomplished snorkeller, down sheer walls to 20 metres in depth or more, over ledges and in the many gullies that cleave them (Site 14).

Pairs of coachmen are a common sight underwater in the Sultanate of Oman.

Pillar Rock

Location: Between Muscat Island and Sidab on the south-east corner of Cemetery Bay. See the Cemetery Bay description for details on overland access (Map 10, Site 12).

Depth range: 8–28 metres.

Season: All-year-round. Snorkelling only, diving is prohibited.

School of fusiliers dart after plankton.

Description and special features: Rocky slopes and ledges border the islet. There is a scattering of hard coral and a colourful patchwork of other encrusting marine creatures in the shallows along with beautiful soft corals deeper down. School of fusiliers dart after plankton on the current side of the rock stack and the crevices house spiny lobsters, curious sea cucumbers, urchins and secretive stocky hawkfish. Featherstars, with their feathery arms sweeping the sea for anything edible in suspension, are abundant here. Using their willowy arms, they attach themselves to any conveniently protruding point. A complete circuit of the islet offers a varied and worthwhile snorkel.

Caution: Even strong swimmers may find this area a challenge and should pay attention to the currents' strength and direction before attempting to swim to the rocky islet from the bay.

From its perch on a purple coral, a featherstar spreads its arms to trap plankton.

Fish watching is rewarding over the varied coral gardens along the Oman coast.

Cat Island

Location: Just 100 metres off the outer breakwater of Marina Bandar ar Rawdah. (Map 10, Site 15).

Depth range: 1–13 metres.

Season: All-year-round, but the water can be rough during winter months.

Description and special features: There is good anchorage in a fairly shallow sandy area off the south-east point of the island. Corals surround this sandy patch so take great care to avoid them while anchoring.

A border of boulder coral marks the edge of coral growth on the south-eastern side of the island. A shallow, well-established garden of colourful

Caution: Avoid the fishing nets around the north of the island; swimmers should be especially careful of passing boats and it's advisable to stay close to the island over the weekend to keep out of the way of speedboats.

sponges and colonial anemones, and bush, table and cauliflower corals in bright yellows, greens and purples thrive in the lee of the island. The variety of corals slowly decreases down the slope towards the sandy bottom at eight metres on the shore side of the island, giving way to the predominant cauliflower coral. Surgeonfish are found in great numbers, grazing on furry seaweed in this shallow, well-lit area.

Towards the north-east point of the island are a number of rocky coves and

Yellow Christmas tree worm feeding on plankton from its refuge among the branches of a bush coral that thrives in the lee of the island.

The colourful, spiny lobster may occasionally be seen walking over the sea floor.

eroded coral channels that are worth investigation. The table and bush corals found there conceal different species of moray eels, small groupers, soldierfish, squirrelfish and damselfish between the coral branches.

Just before rounding the point into slightly deeper water, the rock forms a series of 3–4-metre steps that lead down to patches of scattered corals, which have successfully colonized the sandy bottom. In the shelter of these steps, a variety of sponges, spiral-gill worms, crabs and stinging seaferns can be found. Snorkellers may be pleasantly surprised to see small bug-eyed blennies flicking from rock to rock out of the water, then clinging on desperately as waves wash over them, threatening to hurl them back into the sea.

Large rocks, interspersed with coral growth, cover the seabed around the point. The rocks attract jacks, snappers and angelfish. Groupers and cuttlefish also hide among them. The cracks in the sheer rock face are home to spiny lobsters and lionfish, whose feelers and spines jut out as an indication of life. This site is about 13-metres deep and offers a very good dive.

Cuttlefish can change their skin colour to camouflage them from predators.

Qantab

Location: Right side of the beach below Qantab village. Follow the signs to Qantab from the Ruwi–Al Bustan Road (Map 11, Site 1).

Depth range: 2–10 metres.

Season: All-year-round, but the waters can be rough during the winter months.

This green turtle surveys the reef to set up his mating territory before the season.

Scuba diving gives you the opportunity to explore hidden and unusual places up close.

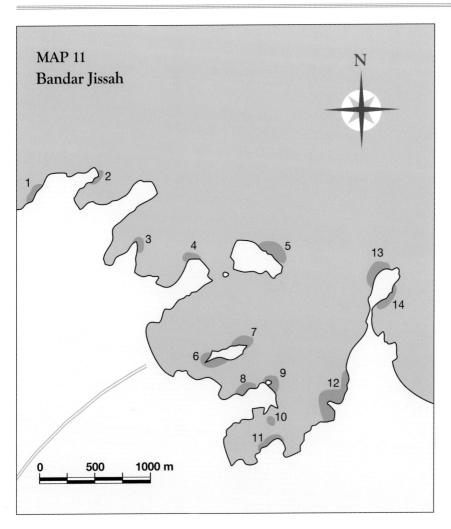

MAP 11
Bandar Jissah

N

0   500   1000 m

Description and special features: The bluff to the east of the bay offers good diving and snorkelling opportunities. The habitat here is dominated by large tumbled rocks that slope down to sand from a rocky terrace below the cliff-dominated shore. A high percentage of cover is made up from both hard and soft corals. Unfortunately, large numbers of tangled fishing nets have killed off much of the coral and about half of all the coral colonies are dead. Despite this, there are patches of beautiful and undamaged coral formations, most notable of which are the huge and unusually abundant large brain coral colonies.

Caution: This bay offers a relaxing dive on a calm day but its position exposes it to high waves in rough weather.

The patterns and movement of schooling fish help to confuse and ward off predators.

First Bay East of Qantab

Location: This bay is only accessible by boat and is easily recognizable by the patterns that years of erosion have sculpted along its western bluff, such as a low arch on the bay side (Map 11, Site 2).

Depth range: Seldom more than eight metres in depth.

Season: All-year-round, but beware of being caught by sudden winter squalls.

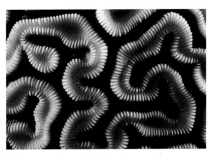

The tentacles of this brain coral are deeply retracted showing the structure of the underlying skeleton.

Description and special features: An archway, half visible above the water on the north-east side of the bay, leads underwater into shallow caves and overhangs, their floors and walls ablaze with the delicate oranges, pinks and reds of teddybear corals. Emerging from the clouds of teeming fish, you'll find the gently rolling hills of the seabed dotted with occasional table corals reminiscent of the spreading acacias of an African plain. Drift slowly along the headland, floating above the hills, which now and then drop into valleys with gardens of large purple vase corals. Moray eels frequently snake their way between the scattered corals and rocks of the somewhat barren surroundings and damselfish busy themselves comfortably near the shelter of a sea urchin or a bush of hood coral.

For those camping here overnight between March and September, please be aware that turtles occasionally nest on the beach, so make sure you extinguish your lanterns after 8.30 pm.

The honeycomb moray can inflict a painful bite if your hand lands on its hiding spot.

Colourful butterflyfishes scout for food near a boulder coral in the Sultanate's waters.

Bandar Jissah

Location: Bandar Jissah is located east of Qantab and can be reached by car or boat. Turn off to Qantab from the Ruwi–Al Bustan highway, then turn right at the signpost for 'Bandar Jussa'. Fishermen wait on the shore to take you to any of the neighbouring beaches – but be sure to settle on a price in advance, agree on a pickup time and pay upon your return (Map 11).

Depth range: 1–17 metres.

Season: All-year-round.

Description and special features: There are a number of good snorkelling and

dive sites at Bandar Jissah, with some easy entry points for shore divers and sheltered anchorage for boats.

The small island off the right side of the main beach is especially good for snorkellers as it is close to the shore, shallow and well sheltered on the shoreward side. The shallow south-west point (Site 6) and south side (two metres maximum depth) are alive with

> Caution: Beware of speedboats, especially when swimming from the beach out to the small island. Divers and boat handlers should also take care to avoid fishing nets.

A yellowbar angelfish emerges from a cave fringed by pink teddybear coral.

an array of colourful fish and corals. Most are boulder corals, in a flattened form called micro-atolls and the sandy channels between provide access for snorkellers. Unfortunately, the emergence of the coral at low tides has caused the centre of these colonies to die and restricted growth to their borders.

This is an excellent place for a close look at the bright colours of corals, cor-

The male largetooth cardinalfish carries its young in its mouth to protect it from harm.

nered parrotfish, wrasses, butterflyfish and angelfish, along with some less conspicuous marine creatures, such as bristle, spiral-gill and featherduster worms and nudibranchs. Each of the curious, flat, brown 'things' you see lying on the sand, which disappear under a patch of coral when your approach, is the feeding proboscis of a tongue worm. Plucky damselfish will earn your respect as they dart out towards you in defensive display of their territory, even against so monstrous and unlikely a predator as a passing snorkeller.

Shy by day, squirrelfishes can be seen at night when they come out to feed.

The north-east and north sides of this small island (Site 7) support large boulder corals, patches of bush and table corals, the unusual and inconspicuous African pillow coral and the lesser knob coral, among others. The north-west slope leads down to a rocky reef, which is some 11 metres in depth and well worth investigating.

The western headland and coves offer rewarding snorkelling and diving opportunities. Look out for sites with tumbled rock, as they generally attract and shelter a greater variety of fish and other sea life. The sea always seems most clear around the headland west of the main beach, where the large tumbled rocks form sheltered pools,

The crown-of-thorns starfish is a voracious predator of corals, living off live coral tissue.

tunnels and small caves (Site 4). Fish concentrate in these pools, showing off their colours to good advantage in the clear sunlit water.

Swimming out along either side of the long bluff that separates the second and third coves west of Bandar Jissah is worth every effort and there is some excellent shallow diving to eight metres to be had along the north-east side towards the point (Site 3). The sheer rock face glows with the pink-orange hues of soft corals, but more impressive still are the beautiful coral gardens alongside. All kinds of fish mass over this colourful oasis in an otherwise sandy desert and many different kinds of soft and hard corals all but obscure the underlying rock.

For those camping here overnight between March and September, please

be aware once again that turtles nest on these beaches, so be sure to extinguish

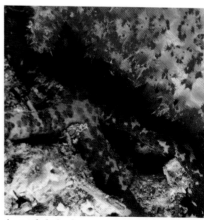

A starfish feeds on soft corals that make up the beautiful coral gardens in the coves of Bandar Jissah.

Left undisturbed, the table coral can grow metres in diameter.

your lanterns by 8.30 pm, particularly during April and May, which is the peak season for the critically endangered hawksbill turtle to lay its eggs.

The peninsula to the right of the main beach separates it from the eastern bay and it's well worth swimming out from the beach along the peninsula's cliff-dominated shoreline. There are several small scenic coral gardens in the small coves leading out to the point (Site 8), though crown-of-thorns starfish have killed off patches of large table coral, leaving large stumps behind. Masses of fusiliers and other shoaling fish concentrate round the blunt point of the peninsula and, below these fish clouds, the rocks are covered by a variety of encrusting corals, and the large grey-green soft coral. Two large rocks lie just off the north-west side of the point and dangerously close to the surface (Site 9). They are also a haven for fish, including large stellate pufferfish that can reach more than half-a-metre long.

The eastern bay, where the Oman Dive Centre is located, has scattered patches of coral. Swim out from any of the small beaches and explore for yourself. For example, the cove north of the small beach on your right as you enter the bay has fairly extensive banks of cauliflower

Cabbage coral is common only in the vicinity of Masirah Island in the Sultanate.

The bottom dwelling white-spotted eagle ray can live upwards of 26 years.

coral and there's an unusual small reef off the south end formed almost exclusively of lesser knob, lesser brain and spine coral, and the starburst coral is well represented too (Site 10). Swimming between the two small beaches on the other side of the eastern bay will take you on an interesting trip over multicoloured colonies of lesser brain coral near the outer beach and knobbed colonies of boulder corals toward the inner (Site 11). The sandy floor of the bay supports beds of sea grass not often seen in this part of Oman. Green turtles feed on these sea grasses, but are quickly scared off by busy weekend boat activity.

Both sides of the arched headland at the Barr Al Jissah Resort offer a number of snorkelling and dive opportunities for those with boats (Sites 12 & 13) as the rocky reefs support numerous fish and hard and soft corals. Turtle sightings are frequent, spotted eagle rays, sometimes in great numbers, glide over the sand skirting the rocky reefs. Electric rays seem to be a permanent fixture. You may also see colonies of the rare starburst coral on the seaward side near the arch (Site 14).

The large north island supports a profusion of sea life on all but its shallow shoreward side, where fields of bush and table corals lie long dead following an attack by crown-of-thorns starfish. The rocky reef slopes down to 14 metres on its seaward side, with occasional outcrops of large rocks (Site 5). These rocky outcrops attract a variety of sea life and are rewarding to explore. Soft corals decorate the sheer rock faces in sheltered places while pin-cushion starfish, sponges, seasquirts and various seaweeds contribute to the confusion of colour in motion.

Colourful soft corals grace the surface of reef-building hard corals.

Bandar Khayran

Location: Bandar Khayran can be reached by boat from the Capital Area Yacht Centre in just over half an hour. It is about 20 minutes from Bandar Jissah and the fishermen there will be happy to take and return you for a reasonable fee.

Bandar Khayran can also be reached by vehicle. Take either the Wadi Aday or Al Hamriyah roads to Yiti and turn right at the signpost for Al Khiran. A winding road leads past the shallow divided head of Khawr Yankit towards Al Khiran (and As Sifah). The first narrow-graded road left will lead you to the two beaches of the south-west cove of Bandar Khayran. If you reach the mangrove-lined shore of the bay, you have gone too far (Map 12).

Depth range: 1–27 metres.

Season: All-year-round, but be careful not to get trapped by the sudden, strong, winter winds.

Description and special features: The beautiful bays of Bandar Khayran

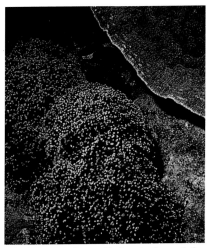

The bean coral usually has its long club-shaped tentacles extended.

provide shelter for a variety of coral reefs and communities unequalled in the Muscat area. To visit these bays without

Caution: Be especially wary of speed-boats and water-skiers, and watch out for the abundant long-spined sea urchins on some shallow reefs.

An aerial view of the east branch of Bandar Khayran, a haven for marine life.

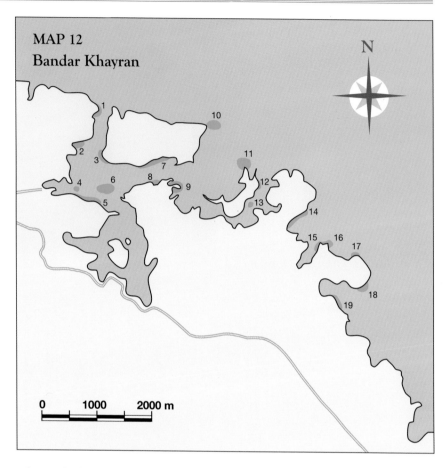

taking a look underwater is to deny
yourself a full appreciation of their
beauty and richness.

*Picknickers' litter partly covers the egg
case of a zebra shark.*

If it is coral reefs that interest you,
Bandar Khayran is definitely the place
to visit. The reefs, which naturally
attract a host of marine life, along with
sheltered waters, create ideal conditions
for safe snorkelling and diving.
Unfortunately, the area is being
seriously degraded by picnickers' litter,
anchor damage and tangled fishing nets,
so if you do visit it, don't spoil it any
further by leaving anything behind.

Bandar Khayran consists of four main
branches. The western branch leads
from the sea through a narrow cliff-lined
channel into the main body of the bay.

The bright colours of these nudibranchs, meaning 'naked gill', warn potential predators of their potent chemical defenses, which compensate for their lack of shell.

Depths here average some 16 metres and coral reefs fringe parts of the rocky western shore and the entire southern shore. The innermost branch is shallow, lined with mangroves and muddy shores and is of little interest to snorkellers and divers. The central branch is exposed to waves and swell entering from the north-east through a wide opening to the sea, where depths vary between 14–30 metres. The east branch is separated by a long rocky island from the rest of the bay and is connected by a narrow channel, which is largely blocked by a sandbar at low tide. This branch is shallow (3–8-metres deep) and has several coral patches and reefs fringing the central parts of both shores.

A grey rubberlips peers out from the shelter of its coral hideaway.

Those driving to the south-west cove should snorkel out below the steep *jabal* to the right (Site 5). A short stretch over barren rock in the inner part of the

When allowed to grow undamaged, table corals form large whorls, sometimes extending to many metres in diameter and are excellent shelters for small fish.

The interesting black-spotted rubberlips school in closely-ranked formation.

cove will lead you over large table corals. Keep on swimming until you reach a remarkable reef – a 200-metre long, multi-tiered reef of large whorled table coral. The upper eight metres of the reef is formed from two species of table coral. Below this to a depth of 10 metres is a fringe dominated by two species of bush coral. This is the sole example of this kind of reef in the entire

An unusual whorled form of the boulder coral, Porites.

Muscat area. Further out along this reef the table corals give way to large fused boulder corals that teem with fish. Take care to avoid kicking or standing on the fragile bush and table corals, and to anchor well off the reef.

A coral-encrusted rocky outcrop lies about 100 metres off the table-coral reef, reaching close to the water's surface (Site 4), offering a pleasant dive, or snorkel for the more experienced. Do not attempt to snorkel on weekends unless you have someone with you to provide surface cover from a boat, as you may risk an accident with speedboats or water-skiers.

It takes a boat to thoroughly explore and get the most from this area as there are countless superb snorkelling and dive sites, each with their own characteristics – far too many to include in this book – so only a few of the better-known sites are mentioned here.

The western entrance offers a dive to a depth of some 16 metres near the mouth off the western rock face (Site 1). There are always a great number of fish here and large rocks with scattered plant and coral growth make this an intriguing dive site that's well worth investigating. The second cove along the same side of the entrance has a reef of large boulder corals and offers great diving (Site 2). Unfortunately many of the boulder and other corals have been badly damaged by nets in the past, which detracts from the natural beauty of the site.

Further into the bay along the western shoreline is a small beach, and diving or snorkelling south of this beach is superb. A diverse and colourful reef of intact boulder corals and masses of colourful reef fish fringe the rocky shore. At one point a platform of mixed coral species – primarily boulder coral – extends out towards the centre of the bay for about 100 metres, before gently sloping to sand at a depth of about 12 metres. The reef is generally shallow (6–7 metres) and brilliantly scenic.

The islet near the entrance to the inner bay is surrounded by a reef, which is possibly the most beautiful in this area (Site 6). It is also one of the best examples of true reef framework development in the entire Muscat area. The reef supports diverse, colourful and largely intact coral colonies, including lesser brain and bush corals and whorls of large table coral in scenic config-urations. As it slopes from one to 8–10 metres deep, it is suitable for both snorkellers and divers, who will no doubt enjoy this safe and scenic site. Snorkellers can see everything from the surface without the need to dive down, and divers can enjoy everything from below, over the safety of the sand, without the worry and risk of impaling themselves on the long-spined sea urchins or sharp corals.

The colours of the fish and corals on this reef are hard to beat, particularly along the north-east slope and shallow south-west platform. This platform is formed from immense boulder coral and

Masses of cabbage coral provide reef fish with ample grounds for foraging and shelter.

Caves offer divers the excitement and mystery of the undiscovered.

extends out for about 100 metres before sloping down to sand at a depth of 12 metres. The islet is small and can be swum around comfortably and leisurely without the need for rest. Look out for porous star and hedgehog corals, Arabian butterflyfish, emperor angelfish and coachmen along the way.

The central headland north-west of the islet has a number of small beaches and rocky outcrops. Snorkelling from any one of these beaches will take you over shallow colourful gardens of bush, table and cauliflower corals, an ideal spot for beginner snorkellers (Sites 8 & 9). The large north island has a number of excellent snorkelling and dive sites. The south-west point has a coral-encrusted slope that leads onto a low flat coral-covered shelf, which drops off steeply on all sides to a sandy bottom at a depth of about 12 metres (Site 3). Swimming from the central beach to the south-east corner takes you along an interesting rocky shoreline and over numerous table, bush and cauliflower coral colonies (Site 7). Large barracuda and small black-tip reef sharks can often be seen in this area.

Further offshore are several small patch reefs dominated by pore coral and fringed by some large table coral. Only four-metres deep, this area is great for snorkelling and offers an interesting and refreshing change in coral formations and associated fish.

The east side of the main island, although directly exposed to the onslaught of the sea, has attractive shallow patches of coral formed of bush, table and cauliflower corals.

A shallow saddle links a cluster of rocks to the north-east point of the island below a large cave (Site 10). The seaward side of the saddle drops abruptly to sand at a depth of 21 metres, down a wall carpeted by bright blue and yellow soft corals. The sand slopes down the base of the rocks to a depth of 27 metres

Dotted spinecheeks are also called 'ghanam', the Arabic word for 'goat'.

These goatfishes are so named for the pair of barbels attached beneath their chin.

round the east side – a good place to see large basketstars. On the southern side of the rocks the sand rises to a tumbled rocky slope and basin covered by colonies of many different corals, which attract overwhelming numbers of fish that will add an element of fun to your dive as they swim alongside you.

The eastern bay is the perfect spot for shallower diving and snorkelling. There are several patch and fringing reefs along the central parts of the east and western shores. A large patch reef in the centre of the bay is formed by a leafy form of pore coral with a fringe of bush and table coral. Patches of porous star, lesser brain and spine coral are also located here (Site 13). Venture to the

western slope to see examples of crisp pillow coral.

A most attractive boulder-coral reef resembling a cascade of mountains cut by deep valleys fringes the eastern shore of the island, just north of the small beach (Site 12). The reef is busy with fish. This is another area well-suited to snorkelling novices and divers. Again, snorkellers can see everything from above, while divers can keep to the sand without missing any of the vibrant life and colours in evidence over the reef.

The north point of the island offers a scenic dive over rock ledges and gullies among schools of fish, including the unusual Gardiner's butterflyfish – an inhabitant you are only likely to see in deeper waters (Site 11).

Bommie Bay

Location: Bommie Bay is the first bay east of Bandar Khayran and access is by boat only (Map 12, Site 14).

Depth range: 1–5 metres in the inner bay, 2.5–10 metres further out.

Season: All-year-round, but the waters can get very rough during winter months.

Description and special features: A sandy beach leads into a shallow bay that is littered with large boulder corals, particularly in the north-west sector. These boulder corals form isolated heads or *bommies* that can reach up to 3.5 metres in diameter, or they are fused into small reef patches. Although a tad shallow for divers, this makes a good area for snorkellers to explore. Spider conches were once abundant here, but are now rare – a sad example of how excessive harvest of an animal can lead to its total eradication.

Against the shore leading out to the first small point, the rocky substrate is covered by a mix of different corals alternating with patches of boulder or leafy lettuce-dominated reef. This extremely scenic stretch slopes down six

Parrotfishes are diurnal and by night cram themselves into crevices to rest.

metres into a wide sandy gully, which is bordered on the seaward side by a rocky ridge that bends away at an angle from the shore, sloping from about three to nine-metres deep where it ends on a rocky reef. The slopes of the ridge are covered by a variety of corals, and attract large parrotfish and groupers.

For those camping here overnight between March and September, please be aware that turtles nest on this beach so be sure to extinguish your lanterns after about 8.30 pm.

Caution: Take care in winter not to get trapped here by strong north winds.

Spider conches are now rare in the Sultanate of Oman due to souvenir hunting.

Soft corals create a surprising rainbow of colour and provide a hiding place to small fish.

Sand Dunes Bay

Location: A long narrow bay immediately east of Bommie Bay, Sand Dunes Bay ends in a small sandy beach backed by low dunes (Map 12).

Depth range: 1–7 metres inside the bay to 17 metres along the adjacent coast to the east.

Season: All-year-round, but the waters can get rough during the cooler winter months, particularly during January, February and March.

Description and special features: A well-developed coral reef fringes the east side of this sheltered bay (Site 15), formed principally from boulder coral, and it is covered by patches of different corals. There are banks of cauliflower coral at intervals along the reef, but parts are largely dead and less interesting. Where the reef detaches from the shore it becomes covered by a lush and colourful garden of soft corals, before yielding to a cover of mixed coral species.

Elegant columnar corals form an impressive approach to this reef.

Between this bay and the headland at Khaysat ash Shaikh, the rocky shore offers many rewarding opportunities for exploration (Sites 16 & 17). There are caves, overhangs, canyons, ledges, cliffs and large rock outcrops, all festooned with luxuriant growths of soft corals and many different forms of marine life, which are alive with fish.

An octopus changes colour and shape flamboyantly during a mating ritual.

Al Munassir Wreck

Location: Approximately 200 metres south-east of the headland at Bommie Bay, Al Munassir Wreck is marked by a large barrel-shaped buoy on which is written 'Danger Wreck'.

Depth range: 12–28.5 metres.

Season: All-year-round.

Description and special features: The Al Munassir was scuttled on April 21, 2003 by the Royal Navy of Oman to provide a wreck for divers to explore. The ship sits on a sandy seabed at a depth of 28.5 metres with her bow facing south-west towards the shore. At 84 metres in length and with an upper deck some 16 metres high, the wreck offers substantial substrate and habitat for the settlement and colonization of marine life – and ample opportunities for exploration by divers. Large schools of fish congregated round the wreck

> Caution: Always be careful when wreck diving to avoid jagged projections.

within weeks of its arrival, mostly grazers taking advantage of the algal growth that marks the beginning of the process of settlement by benthic marine life.

Constructed in Lowestoft, England in 1979, Al Munassir carried tanks and other armoured plant during her operational life. The extensive lower deck can be accessed via two lift shafts from the upper deck and explored as far as the bow doors. Most of the cabins to port and starboard are open. The bridge offers further opportunity for exploration among crowds of sheltering fish in the wheelhouse, ops room and communications room. Some large moray eels have already taken up residence here. Diving on the wreck will surely improve as the colonization of marine life progresses.

The Emperor Angelfish enjoys clean surroundings with plenty of hiding places.

Featherduster worms defend themselves via sensitivity to light, touch and water motion.

Khaysat ash Shaikh

Location: The first large bluff south-east of Ras al Khayran (Map 12), which can be reached by boat and, if travelling by car, Khaysat ash Shaikh can be reached by taking the turn-off at the signpost from the Yiti–As Sifah road.

Depth range: 1–21 metres.

Season: All-year-round, but the sea can get rough in winter with strong winds and rough currents.

Description and special features: The south-east side of this imposing bluff consists of undercut cliffs. Underwater, the rock cliff falls to a rock terrace at seven metres. The terrace is perforated by innumerable holes made by small borer sea urchins, and bordered by a rock-strewn slope. Towards the southern tip of the headland lies an area of huge blocks of rock tumbled against each other to form canyons, overhangs, caves and ledges, teeming with fish (Site 18), and small coral colonies are scattered over these rocks.

The southern shore of the headland is bounded at the western end by a shallow bay with two sweeps of beach, containing a mosaic of flat-topped boulder corals in the shallows. Unfortunately, many of these are dead. However, moving out through them to the right of the bay leads you over a beautiful shallow reef covered by colourful soft corals, which support an bundance of small reef fish (Site 19).

Ras Abu Da'ud

Location: About 10 kilometres north-west of Qurayyat (Map 13).

Depth range: 1–24 metres.

Season: All-year-round, but the waters can get rough in the winter months.

Description and special features: There are several options for snorkelling and diving along the mainland rocky shores – around the islets off the point or over the cauliflower reefs between them. Two areas are outstanding, both off the islets. The north side of the islet provides an exciting drift dive (Site 1), the current of which will sweep you from west to east at a good two knots. Its shoreline plunges sharply to depths

The Moorish idol is easily indentified by its long, white sickle-shaped dorsal fin.

of between 16–25 metres along much of its length and the rock walls are covered with clumps of red cave coral, sea fans and teddy bear coral, while the fish life is spectacular. There are shoals of fusiliers and coachmen, large bold

The endangered hawksbill turtle takes its name from its unusual beak-like mouth.

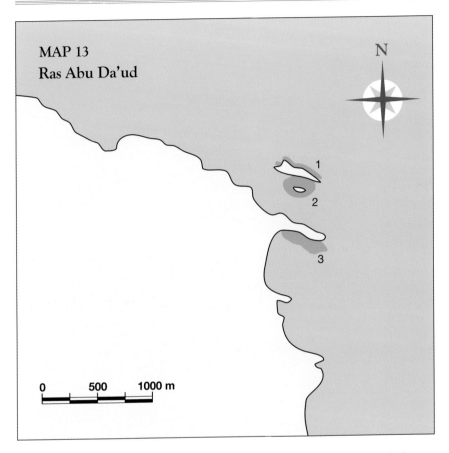

MAP 13
Ras Abu Da'ud

N

0   500   1000 m

groupers and honeycomb moray eels, providing a profusion of marine life. The south-eastern side of the island also offers good diving (Site 2). The rock blocks and slabs plunge to a depth of between 9–10 metres and harbour schools of fish. Be on the lookout for the endangered hawksbill turtles, which congregate here between March and June to nest on the gravel beaches north of the headland.

The islet and rocky eastern spur are extremely important nesting grounds for terns, particularly the easily disturbed white-cheek and roseate terns. Please take extreme care between May and October not to disturb these birds by landing or sitting in a boat too close to the islet and its satellite rocks.

For those based on the sweep of sandy beach to the south of the bluff, try snorkelling or a shallow dive out along the rocks to the left of the beach (Site 3). Fish-watching here is rewarding and also an excellent way of keeping cool.

> Caution: Strong currents sweep round the headland and islet, posing a danger to the unwary.

Cuttlefishes, if approached slowly, may reach out their tentacles to be stroked gently.

Qurayyat Wreck

Location: North-north-west of the seaside village at Qurayyat. It is best to obtain directions from a fisherman.

Season: All-year-round, but the waters can be rough during the winter months.

Description and special features: This wreck is festooned with fishing nets and, as a result, many consider it an unsafe and unpleasant dive. The areas around the wreck are apparently a mating area for cuttlefish, which can be seen courting and coupling in great numbers.

Makalla Wabar or Tiwi Beach

Location: Four kilometres beyond Fins in the direction of Tiwi on the Qurayyat–Sur road.

Depth range: 2–12 metres.

Season: All-year-round, but the sea can be rough during the winter months.

Description and special features: Snorkelling is pleasant off the left side of this beautiful beach over rock ridges and shelves. The shelves have a very dense cover of leathery and grey-green soft corals, and scattered small colonies of hard corals. Bush and table corals, with some cauliflower and other corals, encrust the shallower ridges, adding to the scenic beauty.

For those with boats, the cliffs in the direction of Ash Shab offer exciting opportunities for diving and underwater caves that extend 15–20 metres into the cliff base.

About 500 metres off the right-hand side of this beach is a low rocky reef covered with leathery and grey-green soft corals, some large boulder and porous star corals, and numerous small, scattered coral colonies in 11–12 metres of water.

Although the featherstar appears plant-like, it is actually related to the starfish family.

Ras al Hadd Wreck

Location: A little way north of Ras al Junayz and approximately 600 metres offshore. The wreck is completely submerged, its position indicated at the surface by a series of current swirls.

Depth range: 2–15 metres.

Season: Between October and May/June, before the monsoon weather makes conditions unfavourable.

Description and special features: This wreck offers excellent diving, made all the more enjoyable by the lack of nets draped over it. The wreck lies largely intact and its many cabins can safely be explored. It is a good place to see the Oman butterflyfish, which occasionally cluster together in groups of up to 20 fish; and this area is the northern limit of distribution for this species.

Raha or Hoon's Bay

Location: East of Marbat along a graded road, about three kilometres beyond Wadi Baqlat (Map 14, Site 1).

Depth range: 1–12 metres.

Season: All-year-round, but the season is limited to the inner bay during the monsoon (summer) months between May/June and September.

Description and special features: This scenic bay is sheltered by headlands and a shallow rock spur across its mouth, enabling the development of some of the most varied and luxuriant coral

Caution: Strong currents, made worse by ground swell, can sweep parts of the wreck.

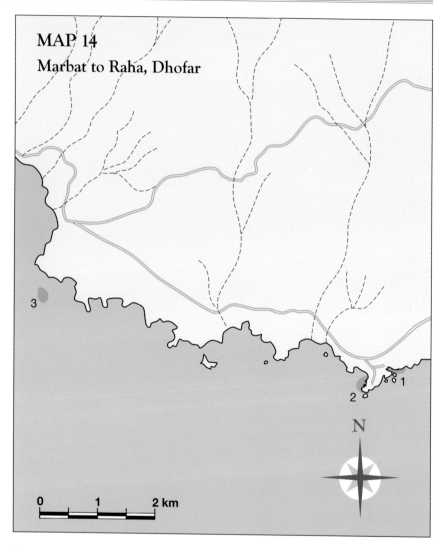

MAP 14
Marbat to Raha, Dhofar

3

2

1

N

0   1   2 km

formations along the mainland coast of Dhofar. The left side has patches of huge table corals that reach 2–4 metres in diameter – look out for the chevron butterflyfish among them.

Continue out along a coral-encrusted shelf that falls sharply to the sandy bay floor and onto a lovely area of coral-covered rock ridges and terraces lying at a depth of between 9–15 metres. Huge sheets of hedgehog coral blanket the rock in places, forming holes and ledges where moray eels and a variety of other cave dwellers find shelter. The colourful colonies of bean coral, which looks more like an anemone than a coral with its long slender extended tentacles, are rarely found outside this bay.

The jellyfish occasionally has bloomed in unusually high numbers in Oman.

Another 'coral' not found in Oman outside Dhofar is the pink lace coral. Although hard and calcareous, this is not a true coral. It appears white from a distance, but the flat spiky fans of the pink lace coral are actually a delicate pink when viewed up close.

The right side of the bay has a terrace with a dense cover of bush coral. The coral-covered slope here ends on sand at a depth of about 10 metres. There is a patch of large-headed peacock coral with hash-marked appearance and, if you're lucky, you could glimpse a sizeable octopus almost completely camouflaged by large boulder corals and extensive starburst coral.

Further out, a rock wall swings sharply left across the bay and the clefts in this wall shelter good examples of pink lace coral.

Caution: Permission from the harbour police is required to dive this site.

The Dhofar clownfish will rarely be seen without its host anemone in close proximity.

Eagle's Retreat

Location: Turn right along the peninsula immediately before Hoon's Bay and enter from the small beach at the end of the track (Map 14, Site 2).

Depth range: 1–20 metres.

Season: September to May.

Description and special features: To the right of the beach a number of rock ridges and outcrops run parallel to the shore. These have scattered corals, large octopuses and crevices packed with stout-spined sea urchins. Directly out from the beach along the shore is an area of rock spurs and gullies between five and nine metres deep, which are encrusted with a variety of corals. This leads onto an area of tumbled rock with large vase corals and tiers of table coral. Further seaward, corals can be found scattered on the sandy sea floor and rocky outcrops. The abundance of fish round the latter can be staggeringly high. Keep your eyes and ears open for the spinner and bottlenose dolphins that frequently pass through this area.

There is an abundance of humpback (shown here), spinner and bottlenose dolphins in this region.

The unassuming-looking streaked rabbitfishes have venomous dorsal fins.

Marbat Reef

Location: The bays to the south and east of Marbat offer many beautiful beaches with good opportunities for snorkelling over rocky outcrops, some of which are encrusted with corals. However, a boat is needed to reach the dive site over the offshore Marbat Reef (Map 14, Site 3).

Depth range: 2–7 metres in the coves, 18–24 metres offshore.

Season: September to May.

Description and special features: This rocky reef averages a depth of some 22 metres. The generally flat relief of the reef is broken by seaweed and coral-encrusted rocky outcrops, which are scored by narrow fissures and sandy gullies. The sea here becomes exceptionally clear in April and May, making for a spectacular dive, especially if large male loggerhead turtles have come in to feed. The rocky outcrops have caves and ledges containing varieties of deep-water cup and mushroom corals, which are rarely seen elsewhere along mainland Dhofar.

This sea urchin is venomous. If exposed, you should seek immediate medical attention.

Raysut Rock and the coast, west to Mughsayl

Location: To the right (western) side of the entrance to Raysut Harbour where the sea wall joins the bluff.

Depth range: 9–16 metres.

Season: October to May.

Description and special features: Parts of Raysut Rock are bordered by a rock shelf, which lies at a depth of nine metres and various parts fall over a series of sheer, stepped ledges to the sandy sea floor at 16-metres deep. The southern side is the most scenic, with deep sandy gullies, caves and overhangs, and huge rock blocks piled against each other. Short seaweed turf, scattered small encrusting corals and seasquirts cover the rocky substrate. A few black corals still survive, but the largest and oldest have been killed off. Some of these corals must have reached a great size judging by the thickness of their bases still attached to the rock faces of deeper caves and overhangs.

The rock reefs from here west to Mughsayl are similar in many ways to those round Raysut Rock. There are large smooth shelves, large blocks tumbled together, gullies, caves and walls with a sparse cover of sea life, but teeming with a great variety of fish. The rock stack just west of the small public beach, and the larger headlands, such as at Ras Hamar (Donkey's Head), are good diving sites.

Fizayih Rocks

Location: West of Mughsayl, Fizayih Rocks are located around a small but prominent rocky point near an offshore islet (Map 15).

Depth range: 2–9 metres.

Season: October to May.

Description and special features: Rocky outcrops off the attractive sandy beaches are encrusted with corals. The hook-shaped rocky point

Oblivious to all else, these porcupinefishes pirouette repeatedly during a courtship dance.

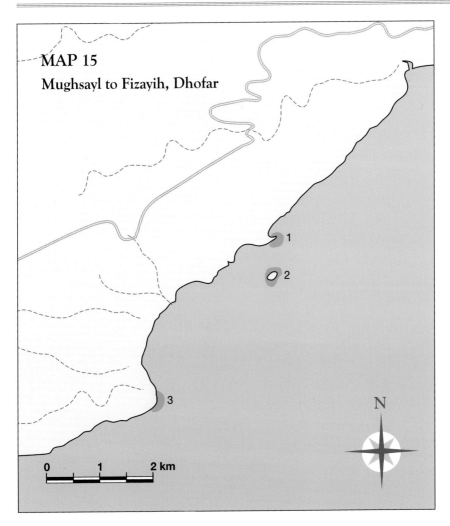

MAP 15

Mughsayl to Fizayih, Dhofar

0   1   2 km

N

gives shelter on the northern side to patches of leathery soft coral mixed with luxuriant patches of hard corals that cover up to 99 per cent of underlying rocks (Site 1).

Shallow, 5–9-metre deep reefs of rock boulders and ledges, gullies and overhangs, over which fish school in great numbers, surround the offshore rocky islet (Site 2). You will also see an abundance of seaweed and a scattering of isolated coral colonies coat the rocks.

Caution: Be sure to convince the fishermen that you are not after lobsters; respect the laws of the country and be careful of the swell in April and May if you are going to land on the south-facing beaches.

Fizayih Bluff

Location: On the eastern side of an imposing and striking bluff that forms the western border of the bay at Fizayih (Map 15, Site 3).

Depth range: 12–24 metres.

Season: October to May.

Description and special features: Between the small stony beach and the point of this impressive headland is a small curve in the cliffs. A cave and a series of ledges well above the water-line are home to nesting rock pigeons and red-billed tropicbirds. At this point the cliffs drop vertically into the water to a rock ledge that slopes from about 8–12 metres deep, which makes a convenient anchor point.

Caution: Beware of currents and be sure to secure your anchor well to the smooth flat surface of the ledge. Fishermen here will get very upset if they suspect you are after lobsters. Assure them that you are only after a good time and that you respect laws of the country.

South of the ledge, an exceedingly scenic area of enormous rock blocks, caves and narrow sheer-sided gullies encrusted with red cave coral, prolific pink lace coral fans, sea fans and a type of black coral with bright yellow tentacles can be found. Fish are extremely abundant – some very large – such as the spotted flat grouper. Although the dive site is relatively restricted in its area, it is one of unusual and stunning scenery.

A colourful garden of seaweeds thrives in the cooler waters of Dhofar.

APPENDICES

APPENDIX 1: WHERE TO BUY EQUIPMENT

Oman's main dive centres offer sound advice and a range of high-quality diving equipment. In addition, several shops specialise in snorkelling and diving equipment, as well as numerous general sports shops that sell a limited range of diving/snorkelling accessories. Some of these shops are listed below.

BluZone Watersports

Tel: +968 24737293

Experienced staff, who know their products well, are on hand to help you select equipment from the wide range offered at BluZone Watersports located at Marina Bandar al-Rowdah. The shop offers the broadest range of brand-name diving gear and accessories and the widest choice of snorkelling equipment. Swimsuits, wetsuits, sun cream, hats and most other necessities are available, as well as a range of gadgets and gifts. Course materials and a number of training guides are also on sale.

The Oman Dive Centre

Tel: +968 24824240

This is a shop for divers run by divers, so you're likely to find someone who understands your specific needs. Located in the Oman Dive Centre at Bandar Jissah, the shop carries a complete range of equipment that focuses on Scubapro diving gear and accessories, Bodyglove and other wetsuits, stinger suits, PADI books, course materials and more.

Al Sawadi Beach Resort Dive Shop

Tel: +968 26795545

Operated by the Muscat Diving and Adventure Centre (MDAC), which also stocks equipment in the Al Khuwair outlet, the Al Sawadi Beach Resort Dive Shop has a range of diving and snorkelling equipment and accessories, although stock tends to ebb and flow with the tourism seasons.

Risail Sports and Leisure

Tel: +968 24510011

This shop is situated in the Risail shopping area, beside the MAM or clock-tower roundabout. It has a good selection of snorkelling gear, wetsuits, stinger suits, and basic diving gear and accessories.

Sumahram Dive Centre, Salalah

Tel: +968 99297494/+968 23211234

This is currently the only dive shop in Salalah. It's located on the ground floor of the Hilton Hotel. It stocks a wide range of the latest diving equipment, including wetsuits and dive accessories. Information on local dive sites is also available.

Other sports shops known to stock snorkelling and diving equipment or that can order it for you are:
Muscat Marine +968 24500483/+968 24500481 Al Azaiba
Ahmed Dawood Trading +968 24712647 Mutrah
Supa Sportsman LLC +968 24833192 Al Hamriyah, +968 24834825 Al Harthy Complex

Appendix 2: Service and maintenance of your diving equipment

Filling your cylinder

For those who are not members of a dive club with its own compressor, there are several other options available for cylinder filling. Most commercial dive centres have compressors and offer cylinder fills as part of their business. Oman Dive Centre, for example, is equipped to provide mixed gas fills. Another easy place to fill your cylinder is at the Oman Industrial Gas Co (Tel: +968 24813012). To find it, drive past the Sheraton Hotel in the direction of Wadi al Kabir, take the first left turn just after the first set of traffic lights after the Sheraton, head down a short road between Mutrah Cold Stores and Muscat Overseas LLC and drive straight through a gateway into the Oman Industrial Gas Co yard.

Cleaning and pressure testing your cylinder

Although most commercial dive centres visually inspect your cylinder, they all currently arrange for one of the following two companies to provide complete cleaning and pressure testing:

Mohsin Haider Darwish (MHD)
Gases Division
Tel: +968 24703411 Ruwi, +968 24626113/5 Rusayl

MHD Gases Division will clean and inspect your cylinder, give it a hydrostatic pressure test, stamp on the test date and issue a safety certificate.

Although the work is done at the branch in the Rusayl Industrial Estate, many will find delivery to the Ruwi branch more convenient. As you drive towards the Ruwi Roundabout from the Sheraton Hotel, turn left beside the wadi at the second set of traffic lights, take the first right followed immediately by the first left turn and MHD will be on your right. Enter through the compound gate and drive round to the back of the building.

Technical Trading Co
Tel: +968 24703515 (Fire-Fighting Division)

Technical Trading Co will inspect, tumble and clean your cylinder, perform a hydrostatic pressure test and put on a date stamp.

Technical Trading Co is the first in a row of shops on the right-hand side as you travel towards Mutrah from the Darsayt Roundabout. Look for the 'CHUBB' sign among the others on the façade of the office building.

Servicing and repairing your diving equipment

For those who are not members of BSAC dive clubs, commercial dive operators in Oman will undertake to service and repair your equipment. The Oman Dive Centre and Moon Light Dive Centre offer servicing of Scubapro and Mares brands and DivEco will service Mares regulators. BluZone Watersports will perform minor adjustments and servicing but for major servicing and repair, equipment is sent to Scuba Dubai – with a 10-day turnaround. Most dive operators use Mares equipment because of the relative ease of servicing this brand locally.

GLOSSARY

Corals

Coral names used in the text are listed in alphabetical order below, followed by their scientific names in brackets. Most names are the same as those used in the *Coral Seas of Muscat* and *The Living Seas* where many are illustrated. A number are included in *Red Sea Invertebrates* where they are listed in the index under their scientific names.

African pillow coral (*Siderastrea savignyana*). This coral is usually found in sheltered bays and on silty substrates.

Bean coral (*Euphyllia fimbriata*). This coral is covered by long slender yellowish-green tentacles ending in a pale bean-shaped bulb. In Oman, it is only found in the Dhofar region and, rarely, in the Muscat area. A similar species has been seen near Sur.

Black coral (*Antipathes sp*). A small slender black coral with yellow polyps.

Boulder coral (one of several species of *Porites*). Called hump coral in *The Coral Seas of Muscat*.

Brain coral or greater brain coral (*Symphyllia radians*). The distinct large fleshy ridges and wide valleys make this coral easy to identify. It is widely distributed, but more common in the exposed parts of reefs.

Bush coral (one of several species of *Acropora*). Bush corals are found scattered among other corals in most areas and can form extensive thickets.

Bushy orange coral – a gorgonian or horny coral made up of stiff slender branches with polyps that appear bright yellowish-orange (called yellow soft coral in *The Living Seas*).

Cabbage coral (*Montipora sp*). Forms large whorls and can cover vast areas to the exclusion of other corals.

Cauliflower coral (*Pocillopora damicornis*). This is a fast growing and hardy coral that often settles first on damaged reefs, carpeting the bottom.

Crisp pillow coral (*Anomastrea irregularis*). This coral forms small domed colonies in turbid waters of sheltered bays.

Cup coral – one of a several species of small, solitary corals, usually found in deeper water.

Daisy coral – one of several species of *Goniopora*. These corals have their long-tentacled polyps extended during the day and can be seen actively engaged in feeding.

Encrusting pore coral – one of several species of lichen-like *Montipora* that grows on rock.

Flat lettuce coral (*Echinophyllia aspera*). Forms flat plates with large, widely scattered polyps.

Fleshy artichoke coral (*Acanthastrea maxima*). A coral so far only known in the Sultanate.

Grey-green soft coral (*Sarcophyton trocheliophorum*). An attractive fleshy coral with lobes that appear smooth when the polyps are retracted but, more usually, appear furry when out.

Hard coral – any of a huge variety of corals that deposit a hard calcareous skeleton, which encases the coral animal or polyp.

Hedgehog coral (*Echinopora gemmacea, Echinopora lamellosa*). These corals form encrusting plates or whorled leaves, which have raised and conspicuous polyps.

Hood coral (*Stylophora pistillata*). This hardy coral forms relatively small bushy colonies with blunt-tipped branches. It is widely distributed from the shallows to great depths and from clear to cloudy waters.

Larger star coral – one of several species

of *Favites* that generally form domed colonies that have the appearance of a honeycomb.

Leaf coral (*Pavona cactus*). Forms small colonies with thin leaves resembling flower petals and is found in sheltered locations with little water movement.

Leathery soft coral (*Sinularia*). This soft coral grows as a smooth mat across the substrate. Its surface is covered by small finger-like projections.

Lesser brain coral (*Platygyra daedalea, Platygyra sinensis*). Called brain coral in *The Living Seas*. Forms domed colonies with very clear meandering valleys and is widespread on exposed and sheltered reefs, deep and shallow, and in clear or cloudy water.

Lesser knob coral (*Cyphastrea microphthalma, Cyphastrea serailia*). A widely spread and common coral found under a variety of conditions.

Mushroom coral – these unattached corals, which resemble the ridged underside of a mushroom, are very rarely seen in Oman.

Peacock coral – one of several encrusting or boulder-forming species of *Pavona*.

Pillow corals (*Pseudosiderastrea tayamai*). These corals include the African pillow coral, crisp pillow coral and false pillow coral.

Pink lace coral (*Stylaster*). A finely branched fan-shaped coral with sharp, pointed, slender branches, found in holes and under ledges.

Pore coral – one of several species of *Montipora*.

Porous lettuce coral (*Oxypora lacera*). This coral forms sheets or whorls generally in deeper water and is difficult to distinguish from the flat lettuce coral.

Porous star coral (*Astreopora myriophthalma*). The polyps are housed in cone-shaped separated cups on domed or leafy colonies. These colonies are generally found in clearer waters.

Purple coral – a gorgonian or horny coral made up of stiff, slender branches with polyps that appear bright bluish in natural light or purple in torchlight and flash photographs (called soft coral in *The Living Seas*).

Red cave coral (*Tubastraea*). Usually found on slopes or in shaded areas, this bright orange coral with its yellow tentacles is unmistakable.

Soft coral – any of several *Alcyonacean* corals whose polyps are encased in a fleshy lobed mass.

Spine coral (*Hydnophora exesa, Hydnophora microconos*). These corals have distinct, protuberant humps spread evenly over the surface of the coral and are found in clearer waters.

Staghorn coral – a slender branching species of *Acropora* that forms tangled coral thickets.

Starburst coral (*Galaxea*). The distinct large cups are colourful, well-separated and end in spiny protrusions, creating a starburst effect that is enhanced when the polyps are extended.

Starry cup coral (*Acanthastrea echinata*). This coral is found in a wide range of depths and forms low domed colonies with large polyps.

Table coral – one of at least two species of *Acropora* that form large, flat, tables of coral.

Teddy-bear coral (*Dendronephthya klunzingeri*). A brightly coloured orange, red or mauve soft coral found at depth, and in shallow areas that are well shaded or scoured by strong currents.

Tube coral – a dark blackish-green, black or brown coloured species of

Tubastraea, mistakenly called tree coral *Dendrophyllia* in *The Living Seas* and *The Coral Seas of Muscat*.

Vase coral – one of two or three species of *Turbinaria* – forms large vase-like whorls or contorted tight whorls. The polyps are seen as distinct smooth cups dotting the coral surface.

Other marine invertebrates

Common names of marine invertebrates other than corals that appear in the text are listed in alphabetical order below, followed by their scientific names in brackets. Most are illustrated in *Red Sea Invertebrates* and *The Living Seas* where they are listed in the index under either their common or scientific name, or both.

Barnacle – a type of crustacean along with shrimp, lobster and crab.

Basketstar (*Astroba*). This is the largest of the *ophiuroids*. It is highly branched and may occasionally be seen by day on corals or rocky walls.

Borer sea urchin (*Echinostrephus molaris*). This fine-spined urchin can be seen embedded in holes in limestone rock or dead corals.

Bristle worm – one of many *polychaete* worms, some of which are long with strong jaws (*nereids*) and others, flattened and covered by tufts of fine hair-like bristles that penetrate the skin and break off when handled, causing an intense burning pain (*amphinomids*).

Brittlestar – the most common of the *ophiuroids*, the sinuous arms of brittle stars are frequently seen protruding from small holes in the reef.

Christmas tree worm (*Spirobranchus giganteus*). Easily recognized by the brightly coloured paired spiral whorls of tentacles protruding from a tube embedded in coral (also called calcareous tube worm or, locally, Christmas-tree worm).

Colonial anemone – a *zoanthid* anemone that forms light brown, reddish or bright-green mats.

Comb jelly – also known as ctenophores (*Ctenophorus*). These small rounded or stubby cucumber-shaped clear jellyfish do not sting. They move by beating rows of hair-like projections called cilia which, when seen up close, may reflect a kaleidoscope of colours.

Crown-of-thorns starfish (*Acanthaster planci*). This multiple arm starfish is covered by conspicuous strong spines and is a voracious coral predator. It can often be seen on or under corals with white patches where it has fed.

Cuttlefish (*Sepia*). A relative of the octopus and squid, cuttlefish are usually seen singly or in pairs as they hang motionless or move slowly close above corals.

Dead man's fingers – a white *alcyonacean* soft coral, possibly related to the true dead man's fingers of the North Atlantic *Alcyonium digitatum*.

Durban shrimp (*Rhynchocinetes durbanensis*). This colourful shrimp frequents caves and crevices and can often be found in shipwrecks.

Featherduster worm (*Sabellastarte sanctijosephi*). Also called fan worm.

Featherstar – one of several species of *Crinoidea*.

Long-spined sea urchin (*Diadema setosum*). This sea urchin is conspicuous for its long, sharp, black spines.

Nudibranch – one of many species of colourful sea slug.

Octopus (*Octopus cyaneus*). Can be seen in or out of holes in the reef and moving along on its eight arms. When disturbed the octopus will jet through the water trailing its arms behind it.

Glossary

Pincushion starfish (*Culcita*). A large pentagonal pillow-like starfish that lacks distinct arms.

Sea cucumber – one of several species of *holothurian* that generally lie motionless on sand like very large slugs. Some species may occasionally be seen combing the water for food with their tentacles.

Sea fan – a gorgonian or horny coral that generally branches out and forms flat coral colonies.

Seasquirt – one of many *ascidians* that vary greatly in size, form and colour.

Slipper lobster (*Scyllarides*). A brown lobster with flat, short antennae in place of the long slender ones seen in other lobsters.

Spider conch (*Lambis truncata*). This is the largest conch found in these waters and there are seven conspicuous spines. It is usually found on sand among rocks.

Spiny lobster (*Panulirus versicolor*). Also called painted crayfish, it is found in coral reefs of the Muscat and Musandam areas and occasionally in Dhofar. *Panulirus homarus*, an abundant species in Dhofar, is a duller-coloured species that rarely extends north of Daghmar near Qurayyat.

Stinging sea fern (*Aglaophenia*). This grey feather-like hydrozoan packs a terrific sting and should be given a wide berth.

Stout-spined sea urchin (*Echinothrix diadema*). This borer urchin causes major erosion to dead corals and limestone and can be seen in holes or channels it has carved out in reefs.

Tongue worm (an echiuroid worm, *Bonellia*). The long forked proboscis of this worm lies along the bottom. When touched or otherwise disturbed, it is quickly retracted.

Fish

Common names of fish appearing in the text are listed in alphabetical order below, followed by their scientific names in brackets. Most are illustrated on the cards *Fishes of the Souk* and *South Arabian Reef Fishes* (both referred to below as the 'fish cards'), in *Red Sea Reef Fishes*, or in *Sharks of Arabia*. Do not be concerned if the scientific name of a fish does not match the one in your fish book, as these are constantly being revised. However, the scientific names are correct at the time of going to press.

Arabian butterflyfish (*Chaetodon melapterus*). This butterflyfish is found from the Gulf of Arabia, around the Arabian Peninsula and into the Gulf of Aden, and into the north coast of Somalia. It is a common butterflyfish in Oman.

Spotted tail hawkfish (*Cirrhitichthys calliurus*). This hawkfish is usually found in deeper water and is readily identified by its black spotted white tail.

Barracuda (one of a number of species of *Sphyraena*). Barracuda spend much of their time patrolling the seaward fringes of reefs. They are top predators and may reach over 1.5 metres in length, but their danger to man has been exaggerated.

Bearded scorpionfish (*Scorpaenopsis barbatus*). One of the more common scorpionfish found in Oman, but often overlooked due to its extremely effective camouflage.

Stellate pufferfish (*Arothron stellatus*). The largest pufferfish in Oman, which has been known to grow to nearly a metre in length.

Black spotted rubberlips (*Plectorhynchus gaterinus*). Called black-spotted grunt in *Red Sea Reef Fishes*.

Black tip reef shark (*Carcharhinus*

melanopterus). The most commonly seen shark and also one found in very shallow waters over reefs.

Blueline snapper (*Lutjanus kasmira*). These small colourful snappers occasionally form schools of several hundred fish found over reefs.

Cardinalfish – one of several *apogonids*, including species of the larger *Cheilodipterus* and the smaller *Apogon* and *Archamia* varieties.

Chevron butterflyfish (*Chaetodon trifascialis*). This butterflyfish tenaciously defends its small territory, which normally includes a colony or two of branching coral (such as *Acropora*) on which it feeds.

Cleaner wrasse (*Labroides dimidiatus*). Look for this black and blue striped wrasse cleaning other fish. It will even venture into the mouths of groupers and moray eels.

Clownfish (one of two or three species of *Amphiprion*). Found living among the tentacles of anemones.

Coachmen – two species very difficult to tell apart: *Heniochus acuminatus* swims alone or in pairs close above the reef; *Heniochus diphreutes* swims in schools, sometimes well above the reef. Called pennant butterflyfish on the 'fish cards' and pennant fish in *Red Sea Reef Fishes*.

Collared butterflyfish (*Chaetodon collare*). Incorrectly called collare butterflyfish on the 'fish cards'.

Damselfish – any one of a number of *Pomacentrid* species.

Domino (*Dascyllus trimaculatus*). Called domino damselfish on the 'fish cards'.

Dotted spinecheek (*Scolopsis ghanam*). An abundant fish throughout Oman's seas, often found over the sandy seabed near reefs.

Electric ray (*Torpedo sinuspersici*). Give this fish a wide berth, as its shock can be powerful.

Emperor angelfish (*Pomacanthus imperator*). A common, colourful angelfish found throughout the Indian Ocean, Asia and the West Pacific.

Fusilier – one of several *Caesio* or *Pterocaesio* species (see striped fusilier on the 'fish cards'). Photograph is of *Caesio varilineata*.

Gardiner's butterflyfish (*Chaetodon gardineri*). Usually found at depths greater than 15 metres, often in pairs.

Goatfish – there are a variety of goatfish in Oman, all of which can be distinguished by the pair of long barbels under the chin and their habit of stirring up sand with these in the search for food.

Golden cardinalfish (*Apogon aureus*). This common cardinalfish schools near holes in the reef.

Grey reef shark (*Carcharhinus amblyrhynchos*). All sharks are becoming increasingly rare in the seas of the world. Grey reef sharks are still occasionally seen in Oman and their tendency to swim in persistently for a closer look can be disquieting.

Grouper – one a great variety of *Epinephelus* species.

Honeycomb moray (*Gymnothorax favagineus*). This is an attractive large unmistakable moray eel commonly seen on Oman's reefs.

Jack – one of several species of *Caranx* or *Carangoides* of which the orange-spotted jack *Carangoides bajad* is most commonly seen. Also called a trevally on the 'fish cards' and kingfish in some areas.

Kingfish (*Scomberomorus commerson*). A very popular food and game fish, kingfish will swim close to reefs near deep water.

Large-mouth cardinalfish (*Cheilodipterus macrodon*). One of the largest of the cardinalfish, and found in caves and under corals.

Lionfish – one of three species of *Pterois*. Called turkey fish in *Red Sea Reef Fishes* and by a variety of names elsewhere, including fireworks fish, devilfish and stingfish among others. Photograph is of *Pterois antennata*.

Malabar grouper (*Epinephelus malabaricus*). A large fish, sometimes more than a metre in length, often found in, or near, caves and overhangs.

Manta – this large and elegant ray with protruding lobes on either side of its mouth can reach four metres across. It is seen occasionally swimming in wide somersaults as it feeds.

Moorish idol (*Zanclus cornutus*). A close relative of the surgeonfish, to which they bear no resemblance, Moorish idols are truly one of the most photogenic of reef fishes.

Oman butterflyfish (*Chaetodon dialeucos*). This butterflyfish is found only in the waters of central and southern Oman.

Parrotfish (one of many species of *Scarus*). These colourful fish are plentiful in Oman. They can be seen (and heard) scraping away at corals with their parrot-like beaks and leaving clear white scars on the surface of the coral, which soon heal if the coral is healthy.

Porcupinefish will inflate into large balls when they feel threatened.

Remora (*Echeneis naucrates*). Called a sharksucker in *Red Sea Reef Fishes*.

Scorpion fish – *Scorpaenopsis barbatus* is the species commonly seen.

Sergeant-major (*Abudefduf vaigiensis*). Regularly schools over coral heads and is readily identified by the vertical black bars on its body.

Snapper – one of several species of *Lutjanus*, some of which are extremely difficult to tell apart underwater.

Sohal surgeonfish (*Acanthurus sohal*).

This is a common and colourful surgeonfish in Oman.

Soldierfish (*Myripristis murdjan*). See blotch-eye soldierfish on the 'fish cards' and in *Red Sea Reef Fishes*.

Spotted eagle ray (*Aetobatus narinari*). This eagle ray is easily identified by its white spots on black, pointed wings and snout, and long slender tail. Eagle rays forage in sand for food, digging deep pits.

Spotted flat grouper (*Dermatolepis striolata*). Also called the smooth grouper in *Coastal Fishes of Oman*.

Squirrelfish (*Sargocentron rubrum*). Called *Adioryx ruber* in *Red Sea Reef Fishes*.

Stingray – generally *Pastinachus sephen*, *Himantura uarnak* or *Taeniura meyeni*, but the taxonomy of rays in Oman remains unclear. The blue-spotted stingray *Taeniura lymma*, commonly seen in southern Oman, is called the blue-dot stingray on the 'fish cards' and reef stingray in *Red Sea Reef Fishes*.

Stocky hawkfish (*Cirrhitus pinnulatus*). A blunt-headed brown fish with bright yellow-green spots, mostly found lying on corals.

Sweeper (*Pempheris vanicolensis*). Forms large schools in caves.

Triggerfish – these fish are named after their dorsal spines, the first of which can be locked into an erect position. This may serve to help wedge triggerfish into rocky crevices and other hiding places where they are safer from predators.

Whale shark (*Rhincodon typus*). The largest of fish, it is not uncommon to see these gentle giants swimming slowly at the surface with their huge dorsal fin and tail exposed.

Wrasse – one of a great variety of *labrid* species.

Yellowbar angelfish (*Pomacanthus*

maculosus). A common and beautiful blue angelfish with a large vertical yellow patch on each side.

Zebra shark (*Stegostoma fasciatum*). Called variegated shark *Stegostoma varium* in *Sharks of Arabia*.

Dolphins, whales and turtles

Bottlenose dolphin (one of two species of *Tursiops*). A large grey dolphin with a short conspicuous beak seen in small groups; occasionally bow rides.

Bryde's whale (*Balaenoptera edeni*). A large whale that is occasionally seen in near-shore waters in Oman.

Long-beaked common dolphin (*Delphinus capensis*). A medium-sized beaked dolphin that bow rides and leaps clear of the water showing a yellowish patch on its flank.

Green turtle (*Chelonia mydas*). A large turtle that moves seasonally along the coast and can sometimes be seen in large numbers.

Hawksbill turtle (*Eretmochelys imbricata*). The pointed beak of the hawksbill allows this reef dweller to reach deep into coral crevices as it feeds.

Humpback whale (*Megaptera novaeangliae*). When the sardines are running, watch for humpbacks feeding on them close to the shore.

Loggerhead turtle (*Caretta caretta*). More commonly seen in southern Oman, this large turtle has an unmistakable broad head and heavy beak.

Spinner dolphin (*Stenella longirostris*). These small dolphins with long slender beaks are the true acrobats of the seas; they frequently bow ride, leaping high out of the water and spinning in the air.

Acknowledgements

We are most grateful to our respective families for their support during all phases of this project and for their comments on the manuscript. In particular, Rod would like to extend his sincere thanks and appreciation to Susan, Josephine and Lauren for their patience and understanding during the many evenings and weekend trips that had to be sacrificed.

Robert is extremely thankful to his family for their encouragement and, together with Joanne Addy, for their company on many snorkelling and diving excursions. Thanks too, to Joanne for her assistance with typing. Thanks are also due to Graeme Hornby for his research assistance during the preparation of this new edition.

The information in this book derives from the study of the entire coast of Oman, carried out over a period of six years by the IUCN (World Conservation Union) Coastal Zone Management Project sponsored by the Ministry of Commerce and Industry.

The Authors

The wild and beautiful coast of Mozambique, where Rod Salm was raised, was the catalyst that sparked an interest in snorkelling, diving and studies of the sea. After leading underwater national history safaris, first in the Indian Ocean and then widely around the world, he became more serious about the need to save the seas.

Rod graduated from The Johns Hopkins University with a PhD in coral reef studies, before moving into a career in marine conservation. He spent the six years prior to publication of this book studying the coast of Oman, snorkelling and diving its entire length, as leader of the Coastal Zone Management Project. Rod's first book was a guide to snorkelling and diving in the Seychelles Islands.

Robert Baldwin moved to Oman in 1988 to spend a 'gap' year before entering Manchester University; at this stage his plan was to read history. His career took a decisive change when soon after his arrival he met Rod Salm and began diving and snorkelling along the coast of Oman, assisting on many occasions with Rod's Coastal Zone Management Project.

As a result, Robert became dedicated to environmental studies and particularly marine life. After graduating, he continued studying Arabian marine life and now works as a marine environmental consultant in Oman. He is author of several other books on the marine life of the region and remains committed to marine conservation.